SONGS FROM 21ST CENTURY MUSICALS FOR TEENS

DITION

21st CENTURY MUSICALS for TEENS

To access companion recorded accompaniments online, visit:
www.halleonard.com/mylibrary

Enter Code
5911-5276-4022-2268

ISBN 978-1-5400-1273-9

7777 W. Bluemound Rd. P.O. Box 13819 Milwaukee, WI 53213

Visit Hal Leonard Online at
www.halleonard.com

CONTENTS

Pianists on the recordings:
[1] Brian Dean
[2] Brendan Fox
[3] Ruben Piirainen
[4] Christopher Ruck
[5] Richard Walters

The price of this publication includes access to companion accompaniments online, for download or streaming, using the unique code found on the title page. Visit **www.halleonard.com/mylibrary** and enter the access code.

ALL THAT'S KNOWN
from *Spring Awakening*

Lyrics by Steven Sater
Music by Duncan Sheik

Hypnotically, at a moderate tempo

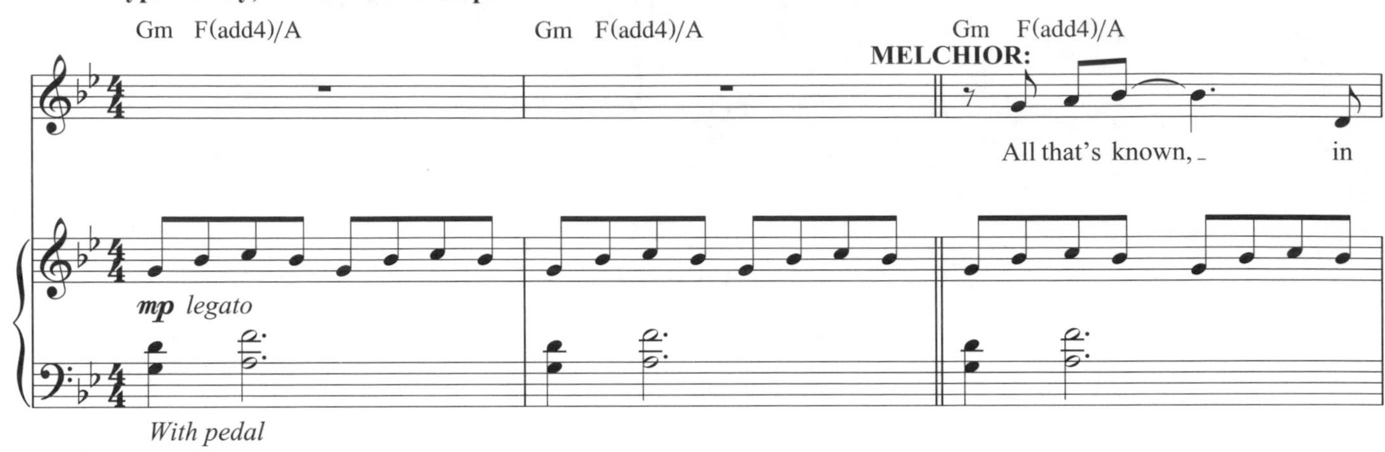

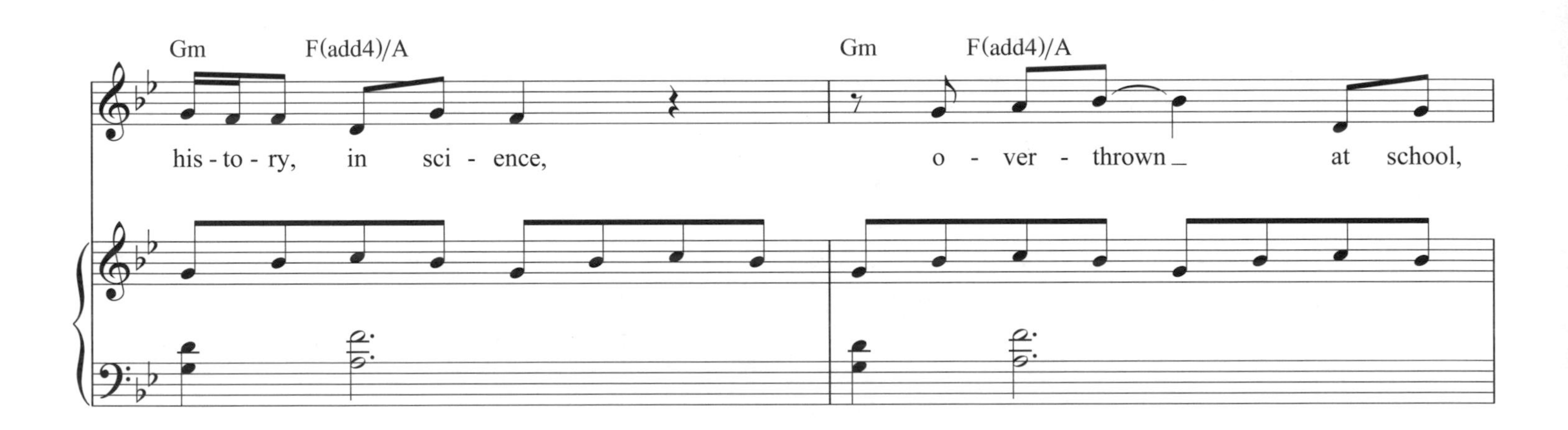

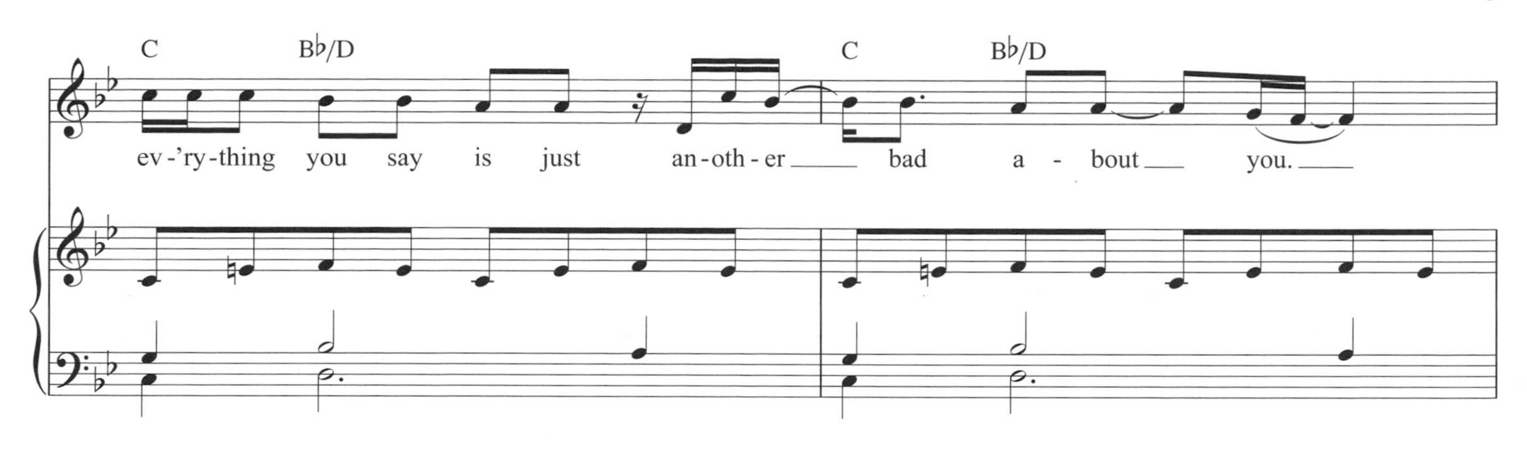
C
B♭/D
C
B♭/D
ev - 'ry - thing you say is just an - oth - er bad a - bout you.

Gm
F(add4)/A
Gm
F(add4)/A
All they say is, "Trust in what is writ - ten."

Gm
F(add4)/A
Gm
F(add4)/A
Wars are made, and some - how that is wis - dom.

Dm
E♭6/9
Dm
E♭6/9
Thought is sus - pect and mon - ey is their i - dol, and

C
B♭/D
nothing is okay unless it's scripted in their Bible.
B♭maj7
Am7(add4)
But I know there's so much more to find, just in
mf
E♭(add2)
Dm(add2)
B♭maj7
looking through myself and not at them. Still I know to trust
Am7(add4)
E♭(add2)
my own true mind and to say there's a way through

Gm F(add4)/A
this. On I go, to
Gm F(add4)/A Gm F(add4)/A
won - der and to learn - ing; name the stars and know
Gm F(add4)/A Dm E♭6/9 Dm E♭6/9
their dark re - turn - ing. I'm call - ing to know the world's true yearn - ing, the
C B♭/D C B♭/D
hun - ger that a child feels for ev - 'ry - thing they're shown.
cresc. poco a poco

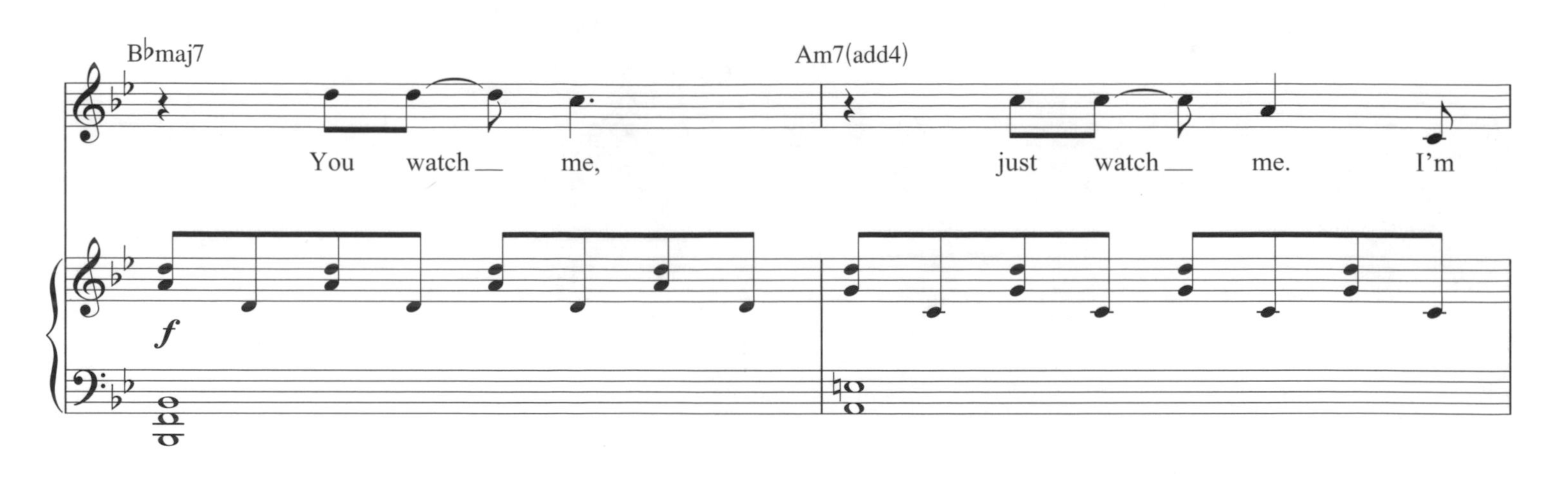
B♭maj7
Am7(add4)
You watch me, just watch me. I'm
f

E♭(add2)
Dm(add2)
B♭maj7
call - ing, and one day all will know. You watch me,

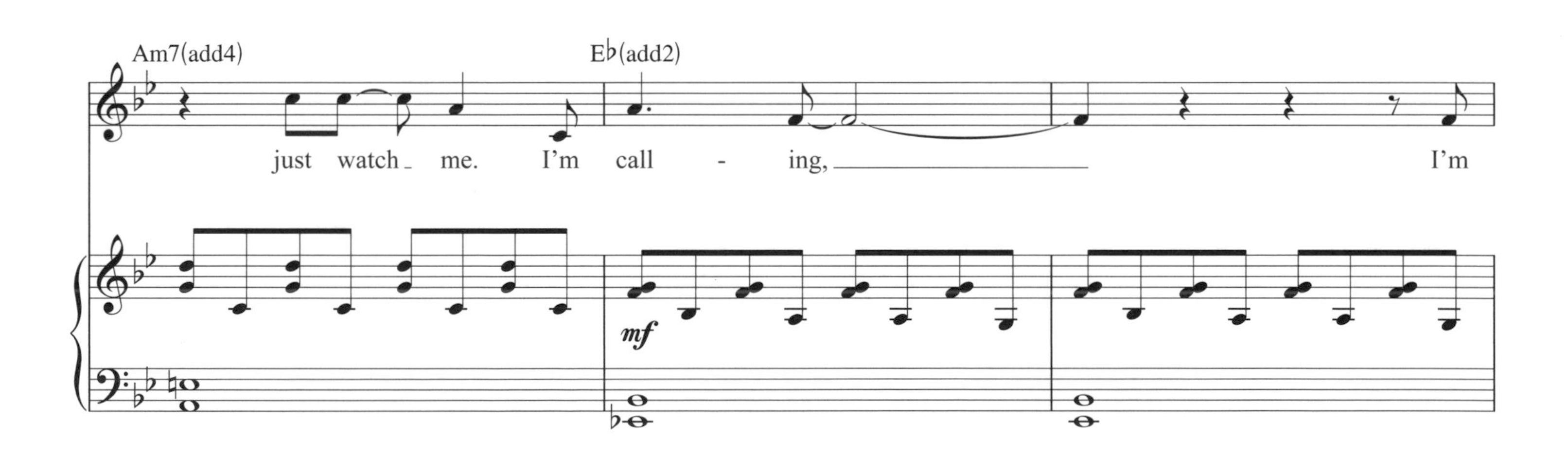
Am7(add4)
E♭(add2)
just watch me. I'm call - ing, I'm
mf

Dm9/G
call - ing, and one day all will know...

EVERYTHING TO WIN

from *Anastasia*

Lyrics by Lynn Ahrens
Music by Stephen Flaherty

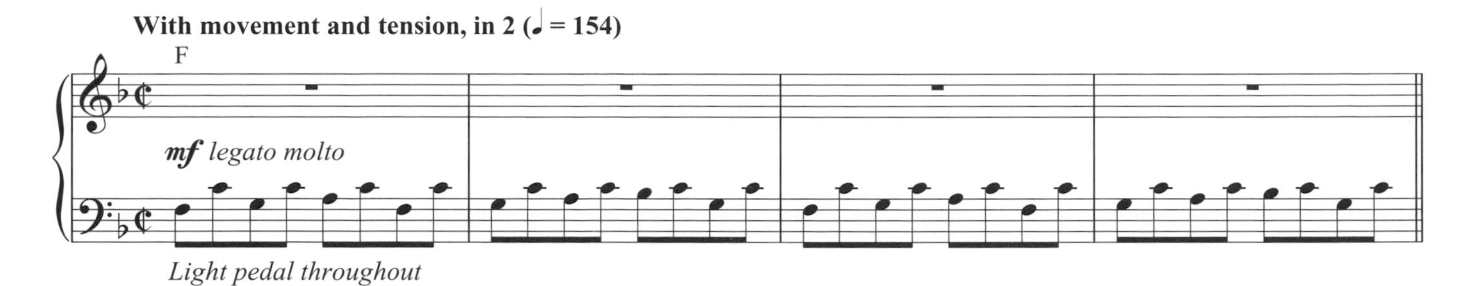

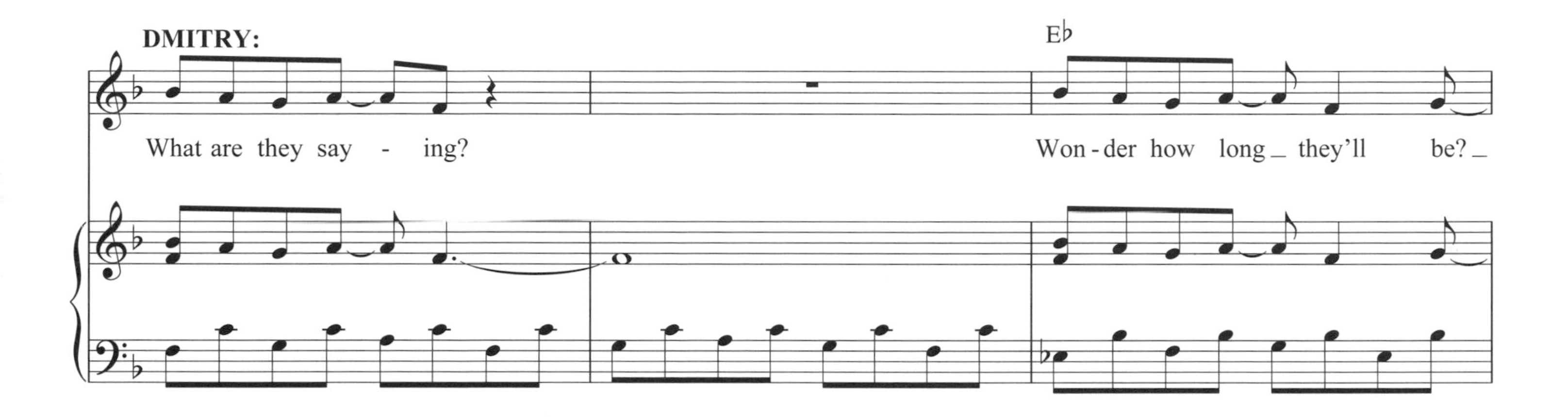

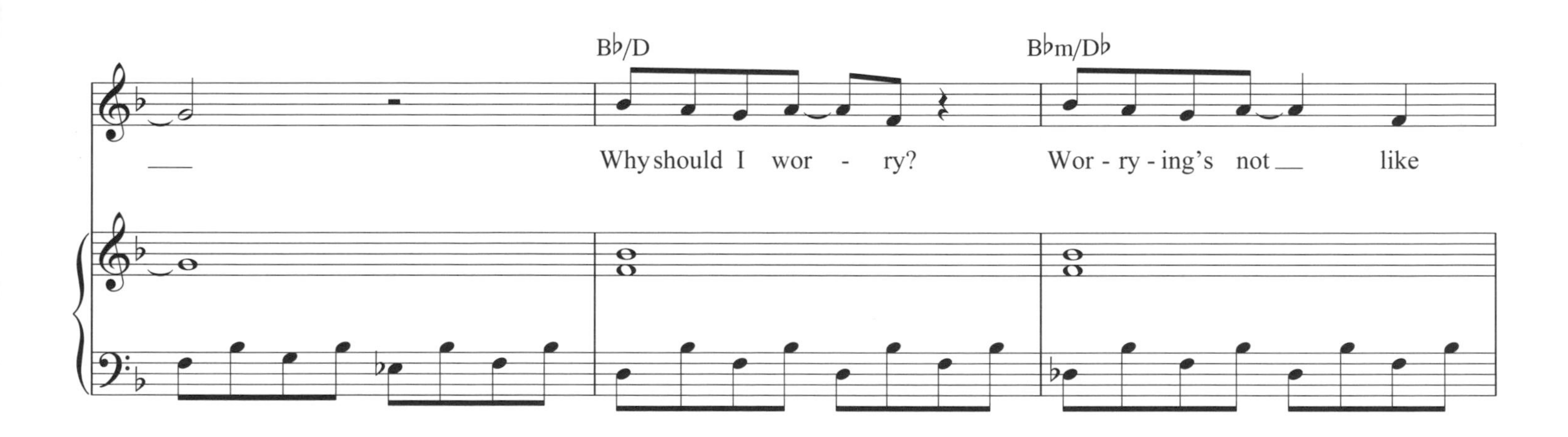

B♭/D
B♭m/D♭
F/C
G7/B
pace and stew and wait till the girl walks in.
Gm7
F(add2)/A
C7sus
Why pan - ic now with ev - 'ry - thing to
F
win?
C7sus
cresc.
F
mf
Noth - ing but si - lence. This could be bad, but

E♭6
no! Let's as - sume it's good.
B♭/D
Thought it was fool - proof.
B♭m/D♭
Noth - ing is fool - proof!
Fsus
F
Whoa! Bet - ter knock on wood!
E♭maj9
Girl gets a fam - 'ly,
B♭/D
boy gets rich and
B♭m/D♭
F/C
fair - y - tale gets a spin!
G7/B
Gm7
F(add2)/A
How can we fail with

C7sus
F
ev - 'ry - thing to win?
I won - der
cresc.
E♭maj9
B♭/D
B♭
F
if our paths will ev - er cross a - gain
f
Am
Dm
Dm/C
the way they did when you were eight and I was ten.
G7/B
B♭sus2
We said this was good - bye

F5/A
Dm
Am7/C
Bm7♭5
but e - ven so, you
E♭9♯11
E♭7
E♭13
E♭9
Gm/C
C
nev - er know. You nev - er know.
cresc. poco a poco
8vb
C9sus
C
C9sus
C6
C9sus
C
Dm/C
Gm/C
cresc. molto
(8vb)
C9sus
Simply (quasi-rubato)
Fsus
F
I should be glad that
6
fp
p
(8vb)

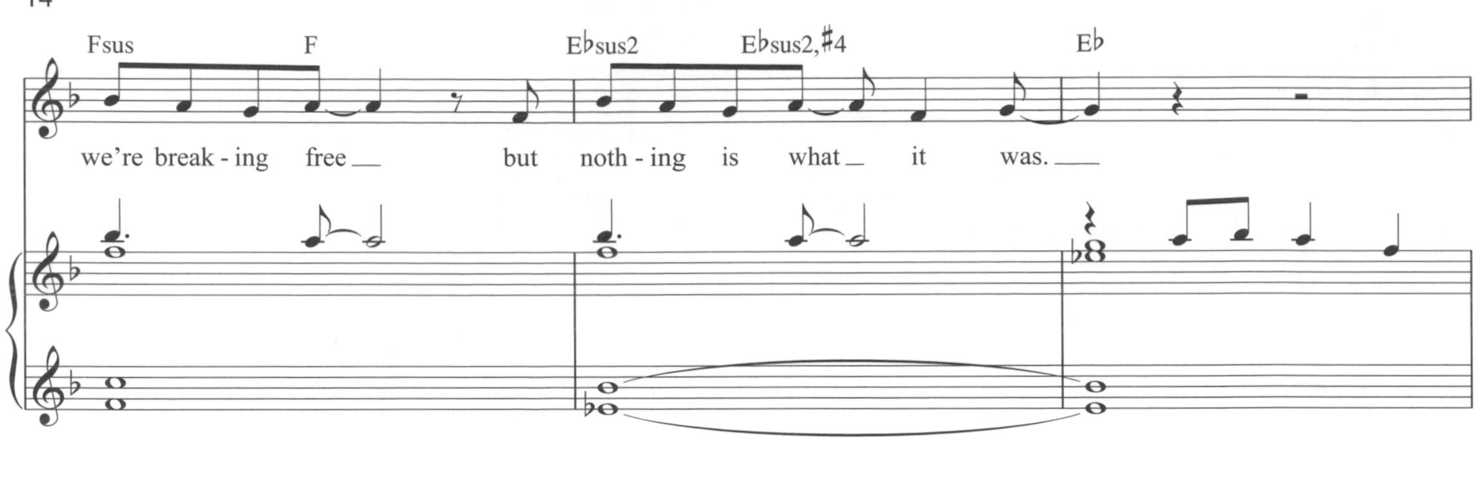
Fsus
F
E♭sus2
E♭sus2,♯4
E♭
we're break - ing free
but noth - ing is what it was.

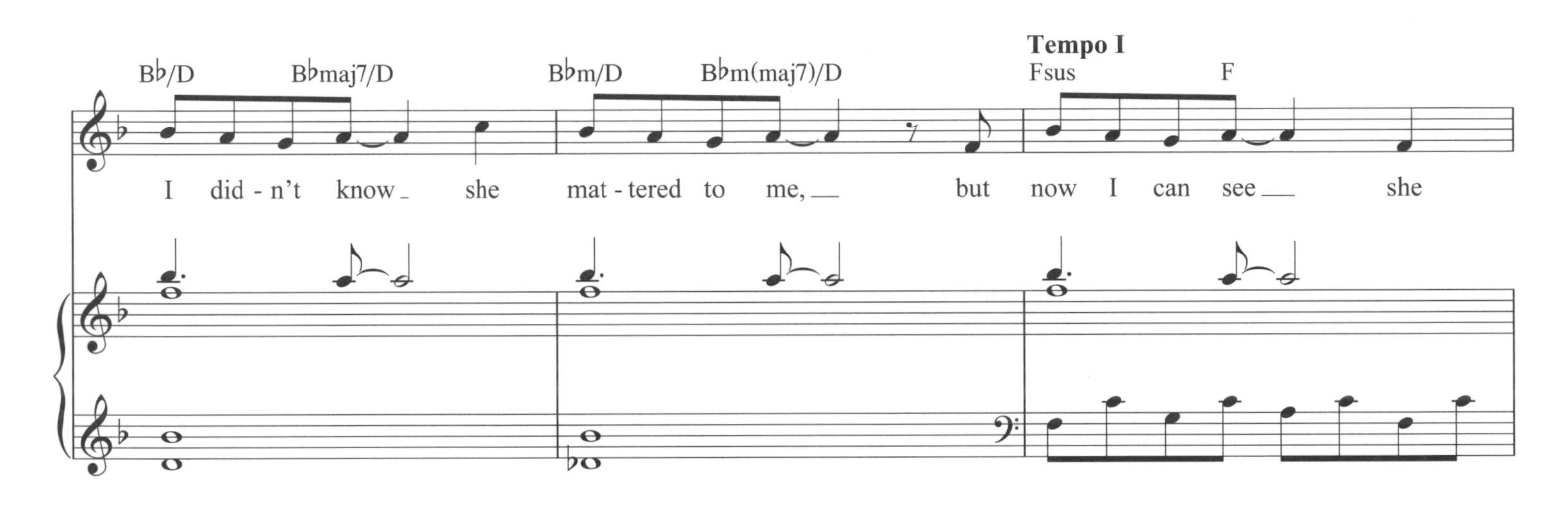
Tempo I
B♭/D
B♭maj7/D
B♭m/D
B♭m(maj7)/D
Fsus
F
I did - n't know she mat - tered to me, but now I can see she

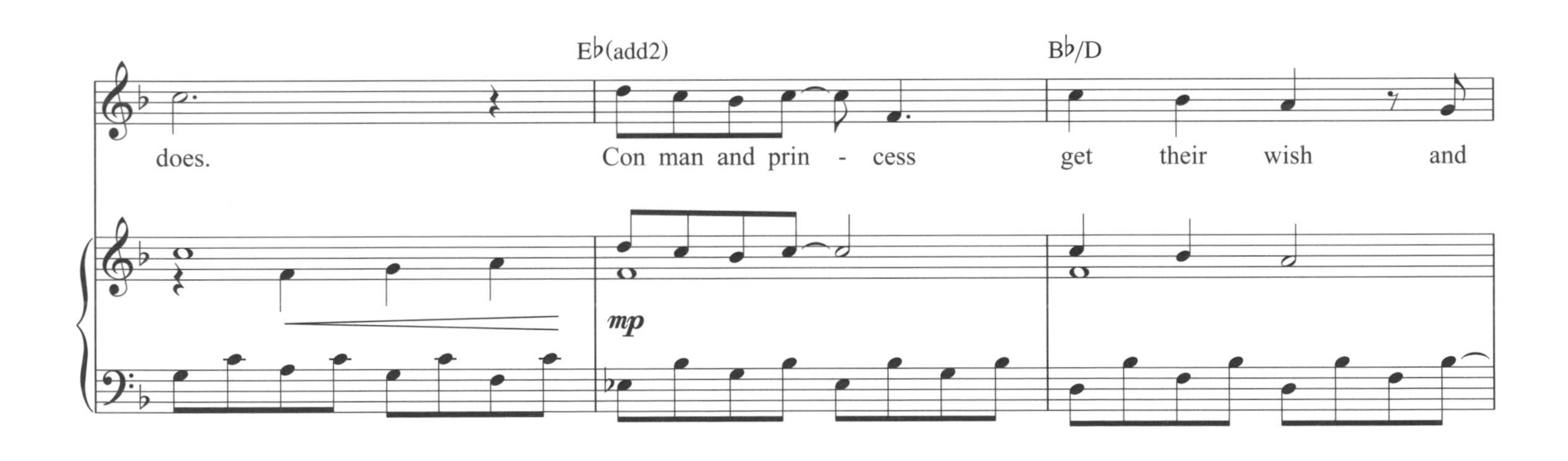
E♭(add2)
B♭/D
does. Con man and prin - cess get their wish and
mp

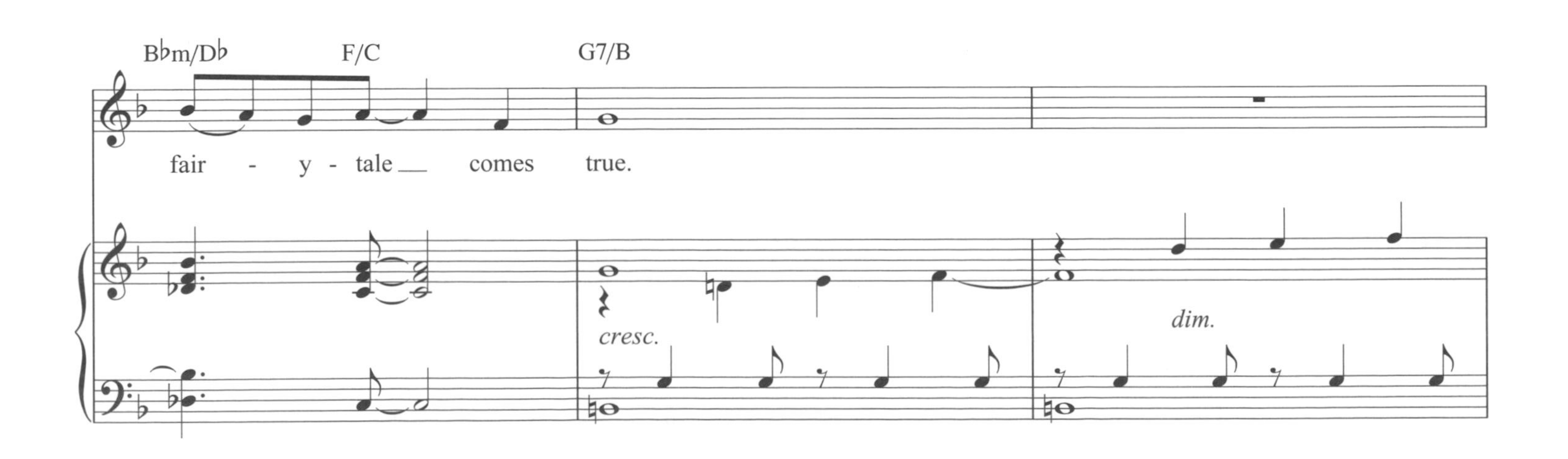
B♭m/D♭
F/C
G7/B
fair - y - tale comes true.
cresc.
dim.

Freely
More deliberately, in 4
Gm7
F(add2)/A
C7sus
Dm
Fun - ny, the one small part I nev - er knew,
mp
colla voce
cresc.
Dm/C
Gm7
C7sus
C/B♭
with ev - 'ry - thing to win, the
mf
Am7
D7sus
D7
G7sus
F(add2)/A
on - ly thing I lose
mp cresc.
Freely
C13sus
F
poco rit.
is you.
mf
poco rit.
mp

FOR FOREVER
from *Dear Evan Hansen*

Music and Lyrics by Benj Pasek
and Justin Paul

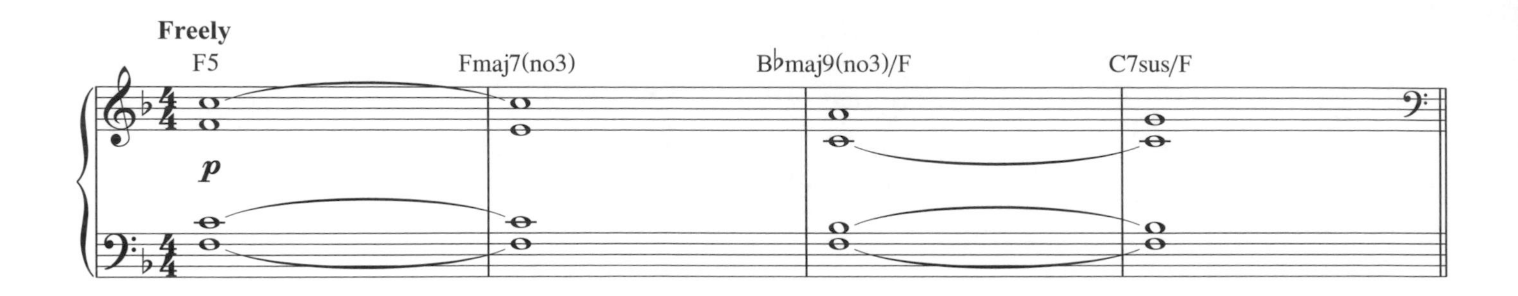

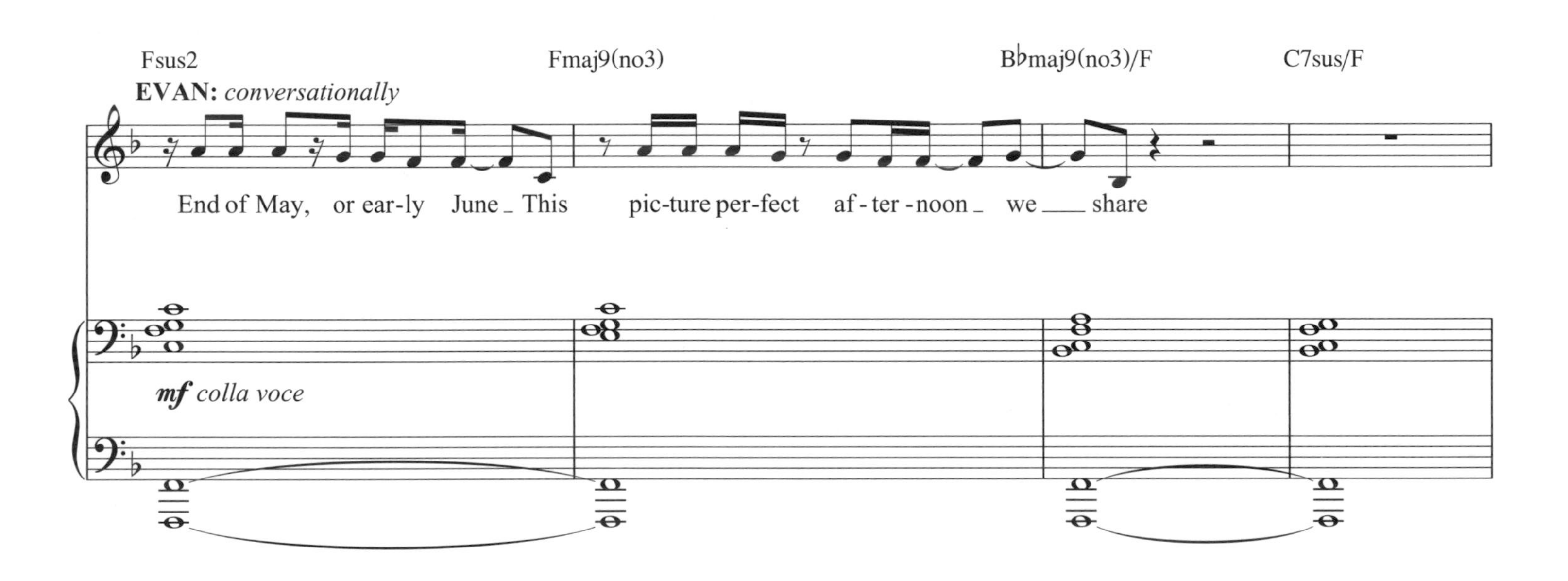

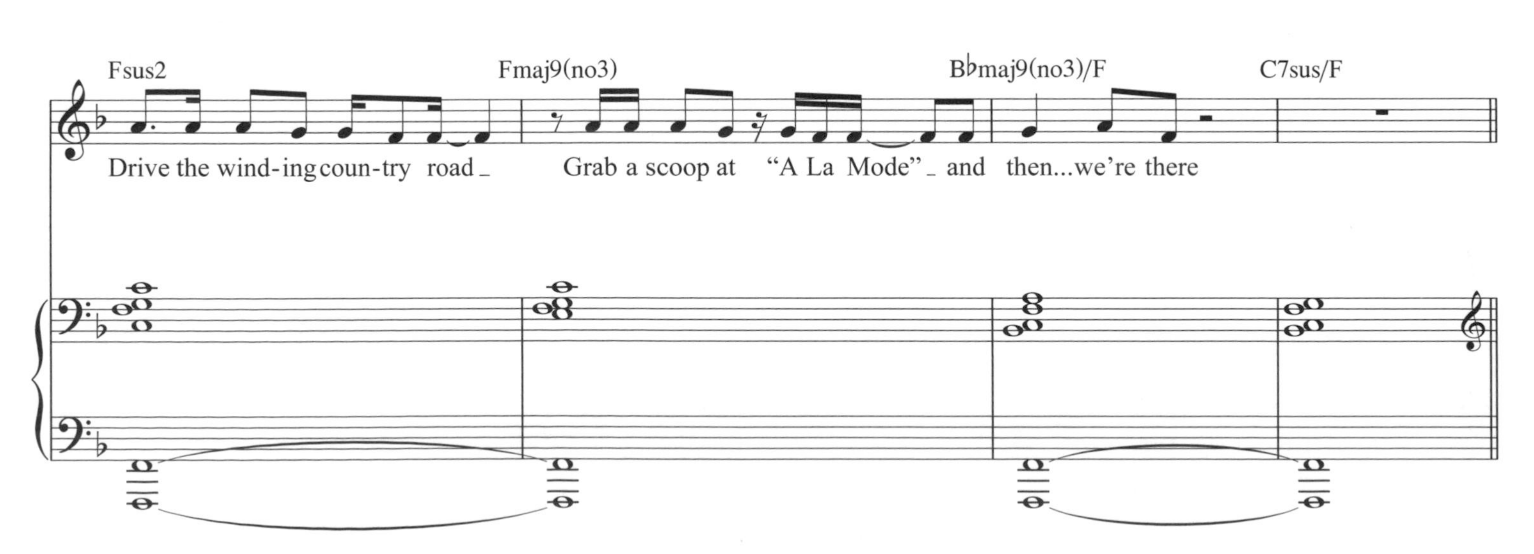

B♭sus2
An o - pen field that's framed with trees We pick a spot and shoot the breeze like
Fsus2
B♭sus2
B♭maj9(no3)
bud-dies do Quot-ing songs by our fa-v'rite bands Tell-ing jokes no one un-der-stands ex-
Fsus2
Dm
B♭
C(add4)
cept us two And we talk and take in the view
In time (♩ = 91)
F5
Fmaj7(no3)
F/A
B♭sus2
All we see is sky for for-ev-er We
With pedal

F5
Fmaj7(no3)
F/A
B♭sus2
let the world pass by
for for-ev-er
Dm7(no5)
F5/C
B♭sus2
F/A
Feels like we could go on
for for-ev-er this way
G7(add4)
F/B♭
C(add4)
Più mosso (♩ = 97)
Fsus2
Two friends
on a per-fect day
Fmaj9(no3)
B♭maj9(no3)/F
C7sus/F
We

Fsus2
Fmaj9(no3)
walk a-while and talk a-bout the things we'll do when we get out of
B♭maj9(no3)/F
Fsus2
school
Bike the Ap-pa-la-chian Trail, or
Fmaj9(no3)
B♭maj9(no3)/F
write a book, or learn to sail Would-n't that be cool? There's
B♭sus2
noth-ing that we can't dis-cuss Like, girls we wish would no-tice us but

Fsus2
F
Fmaj9(no3)/A
B♭sus2
B♭sus2,♯4
nev - er do
He looks a - round and says to me "There's
B♭(add2)
Fsus2
F
Dm
B♭
no-where else I'd rath-er be" And I say "Me too"
And we talk and take in the view
C(add4)
Dm
B♭
C(add4)
We just talk and take in the view
p
Hold back (♩ = 96)
F5
F5/E
F5/A
B♭sus2
All we see is sky for for - ev - er We
mf

F5
F5/E
F5/A
B♭sus2
let the world pass by
for for - ev - er
sim.
Dm7(no5)
F5/C
B♭sus2
F5/A
Feels like we could go on
for for - ev - er this way
E♭maj9
F/B♭
this
way
F5
F5/E
F5/A
B♭sus2
All we see is light
for for - ev - er

F5
F5/E
F5/A
B♭sus2
'Cause the sun shines bright for for-ev-er
Dm7(no5)
C(add4)
B♭sus2
F5/A
Like we'll be al - right for for-ev-er this way
G7(add4)
B♭maj9(no3)
C(add4)
F5
accel.
Two friends on a per-fect day And
accel.
Faster (♩ = 99)
D♭(add2)
A♭/C
Fm7
E♭(add4)
there he goes, rac-in' toward the tall - est tree From
f

D♭(add2)
A♭/C
Fm7
E♭(add4)
far a-cross a yel-low field I hear him call-in' "Fol-low me!"
sim.
E♭sus2
B♭/D
Gm7
Fsus
There we go wonder-in' how the world might look from up so high
Picking up speed (♩ = 100)
E♭sus2
One foot af - ter the oth-er One branch then to an-oth-er
mf sub.
F(add4)
I climb high - er and high-er I climb 'til the en-tire
cresc. poco a poco

Gm
Eb
F/Eb
rall.
sun shines on my face
f
rall.
Eb(add2)
Gm
F
Bbsus2/D
Ebsus2
And I sud-den-ly feel the branch give way I'm on the ground
mf colla voce
Slower
Bb/F
Dm/G
Gm
Bb/F
My arm goes numb I look a-round and I see him
p
C9sus
C9(add4)
Eb
F(add4)
come to get me He's come to get me And ev-'ry-thing's o-kay

In time, slowly (♩ = 84)
G5
Gmaj7(no3)
G5/B
Csus2
Picking up
All we see is sky for forever We let the world pass by
for forever
G5/E
Gmaj7(no3)/D
accel. poco a poco
Csus2
G(add4)/B
Bud dy, you and I for forever this way
mf accel. poco a poco
Fmaj9
Cmaj9(no3)
this way
f
A tempo (♩ = 96)
G5/F♯
All we see is light
ff
sim.

G5
G5/F♯
G5/B
G5/C
'Cause the sun burns bright
G5/E
Gmaj7(no3)/D
C(add2)
G5/B
A7(add4)
We could be al - right for for-ev-er this way
p sub.
Am11
Cmaj9(no3)
D7(no3)
In time, slowly (♩ = 86)
Gsus2
Two friends True friends on a per fect day
colla voce
mp
Gmaj9(no3)
Cmaj9(no3)/G
D7sus/G
G5
rall.
L.H.
mf
rall.

I BELIEVE

from the Broadway Musical *The Book of Mormon*

Words and Music by Trey Parker,
Robert Lopez and Matt Stone

Chorus parts have been omitted from this solo voice edition.

F5
Bb2
C
Dm7
lowed my faith to be shak - en. Oh, what's the mat-ter with me? I've al-ways
Db
Eb/Db
Cm7
Fm7
longed to help the need - y, to do the things I nev - er dared.
Db
Eb/Db
C
rit.
Fm
This was the time for me to step up, so then why was I so scared? A
rit.
Più mosso (colla voce)
C7
F6
C7
C#dim7
F6
war-lord who shoots peo-ple in the face. What's so scar-y a-bout that? I must

Broadly
C
C/B♭
F5/A
G
G/B
C
trust that my Lord is might - i - er, and al - ways has my back. Now I
Steady pop, in 4 (♩ = 82)
D♭
cresc. poco a poco
E♭/D♭
D♭(♭5)/C
must be com - plete - ly de - vout. I can't have e - ven one shred of
cresc. poco a poco
Csus
C
mf
F
C/F
doubt! I be - lieve ___ that the
mf
B♭/F
C/F
C/E
Dm7
Am7
Lord God cre - at - ed the u - ni - verse. I be - lieve ___ that he sent his on - ly Son to die ___
sim.

B♭maj7 C C♯dim7 E♭(♭9)/F B♭/F B♭ F/A G7
for my sins, and I be - lieve that an - cient Jews built boats and sailed to A - mer - i - ca.
N.C. C7sus
f
I am a Mor - mon, and a Mor - mon just be -
f
F5 C5/G mp F5 C5/G
lieves. You can - not just be - lieve part way, you
mp
F5 C5/G F5 B♭2
have to be - lieve in it all. My prob - lem was doubt - ing the Lord's will in -

C
Dm7
Db
Eb/Db
stead of stand - ing tall. I can't al - low my-self to have an - y doubt. It's time to
Cm7
Fm7
Db
cresc. poco a poco
Eb/Db
set my wor - ries free. Time to show the world what El - der Price is a - bout, and
cresc. poco a poco
Dbmaj7/C
Csus
C
mf
F
C/F
share the pow-er in - side of me! I be - lieve that
mf
Bb/F
C/F
C/E
Dm7
Am7
God has a plan for all of us. I be - lieve that plan in - volves

B♭maj9 C C♯dim7 E♭9/F B♭/F
me get-ting my own plan-et. And I be - lieve that the cur-rent pres - i - dent of the church, Thom-as
3
B♭ F/A G7 N.C.
Mon - son, speaks di - rect - ly to God. I am a Mor - mon, and,
C7 F9
dang it, a Mor - mon just be - lieves. I
A♭ B♭ Gm7 Cm7
know that I must go and do the things my God com - mands. I
sim.

A♭ B♭ C A♭ B♭/A♭
re - al - ize now why he sent me here! If you ask the Lord in faith, he will
Gm7 Cm7 A♭ B♭/A♭ C
al - ways an - swer you. Just be - lieve in him and have no fear.
sub. mp
8vb
D♭
f
I be - lieve
f
G♭ D♭/G♭ C♭/G♭ D♭/G♭ D♭/F E♭m7 B♭m7
that Sa - tan has a hold of you. I be - lieve that the Lord
mf

C♭maj7
D♭
Ddim7
D♭m/G♭
C♭/G♭
God has sent _ me here. And I be - lieve that in nine-teen sev-en-ty-eight God
mf
C♭
G♭/B♭
A♭7
N.C.
changed his mind _ a-bout black peo-ple. _
You can be a Mor-mon,
mf
D♭7sus
G♭5
a Mor-mon who just be - lieves.
mp
And
f
mp
D♭5/A♭
G♭/B♭
D♭5/A♭
now I can feel _ the ex - cite-ment. This is the mo-ment I was born to do. _ And I

G♭5
C♭2
D♭
E♭m7
feel so in - cred - i - ble to be shar-ing my faith with you. The
D
E/D
C♯m7
F♯m7
cresc. poco a poco
scrip-tures say that if you ask in faith, if you ask God him-self, you'll know. But you
cresc. poco a poco
D9
E/D
Bm/C♯
must ask him with - out an - y doubt and let your spir - it
C♯sus
C♯
G♭
D♭/G♭
f
grow. I be - lieve that
f

C♭/G♭ D♭/G♭ D♭/F E♭m7 B♭m7
God lives on a plan-et called Ko-lob. I be-lieve that Je-sus has
C♭maj7 C♭ D♭ Ddim7 F♭9/G♭ C♭/G♭
his own plan-et as well. And I be-lieve that the Gar-den of E-den was in
C♭ G♭/B♭ A♭ Em/G
mp
Jack-son Coun-ty, Mis-sou-ri. If you be-lieve, the Lord will re-veal it. And you'll
mp
C♯m7 N.C.
know it's all true, you'll just feel it. You'll be a Mor-mon, and,

D♭7sus
f
by gosh, a Mor - mon just be -
C♭/D♭ D♭ C♭/D♭ D♭
G♭ D♭/G♭
lieves.
C♭/G♭ G♭ D♭9/G♭ D♭/G♭
Oh, I be - lieve.
ff
E♭m7 B♭m7
C♭ G♭/C♭ D♭9
rall.
I be - lieve!
N.C.
G♭

ONE STEP CLOSER

from *The Little Mermaid - A Broadway Musical*

Music by Alan Menken
Lyrics by Glenn Slater

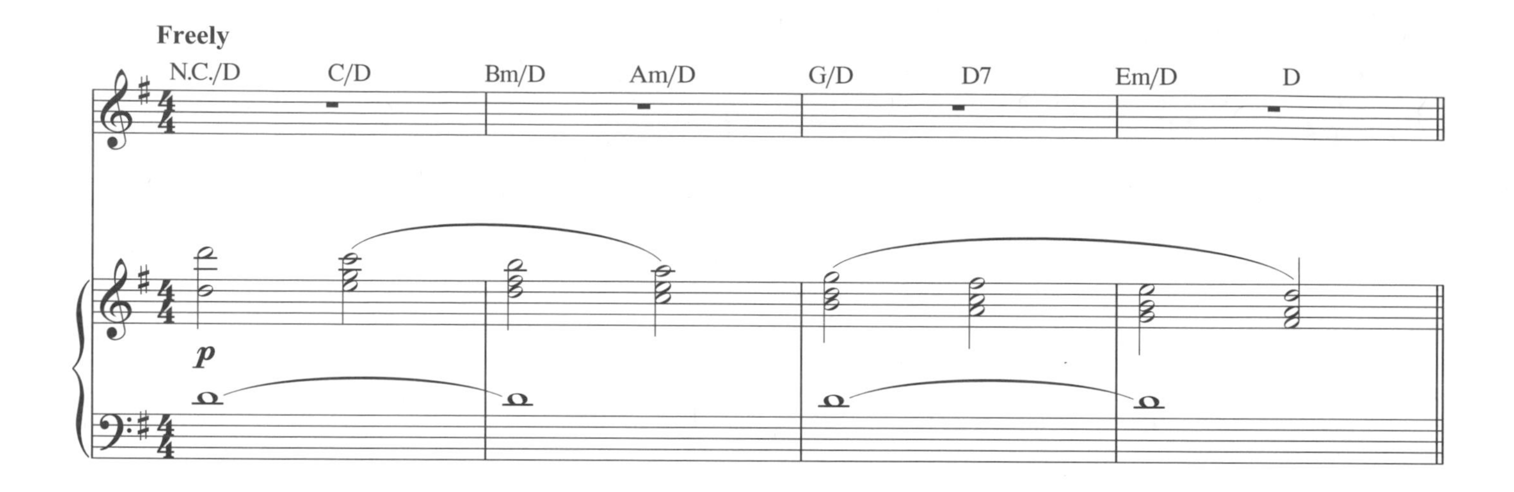

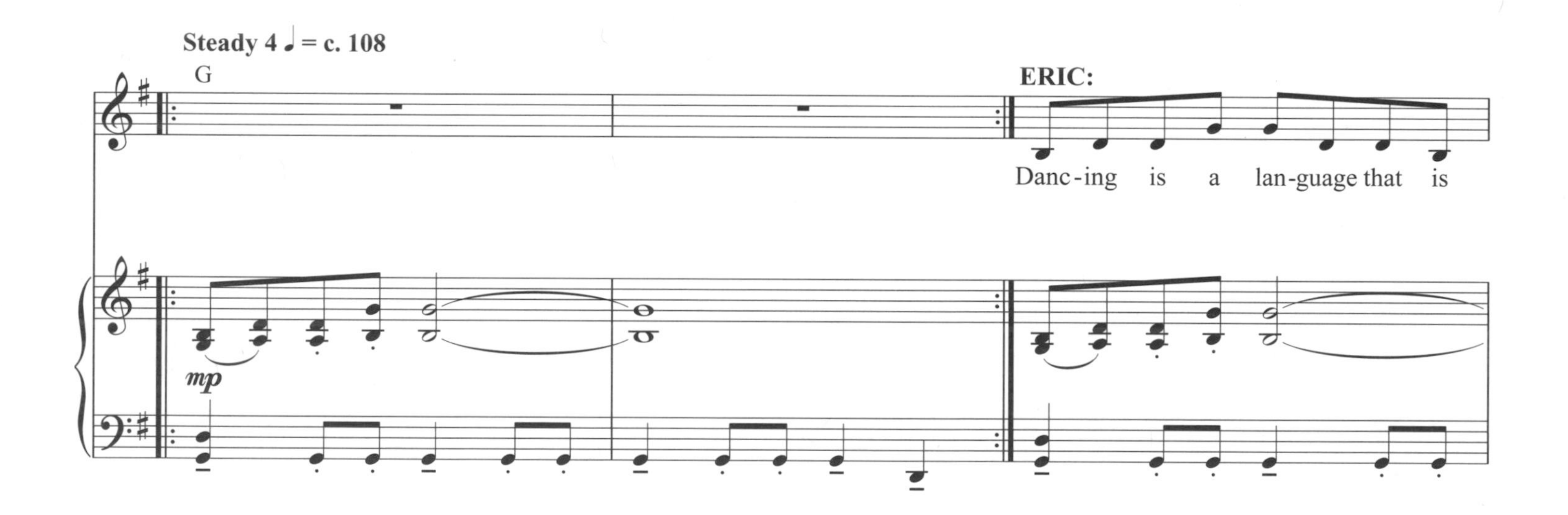

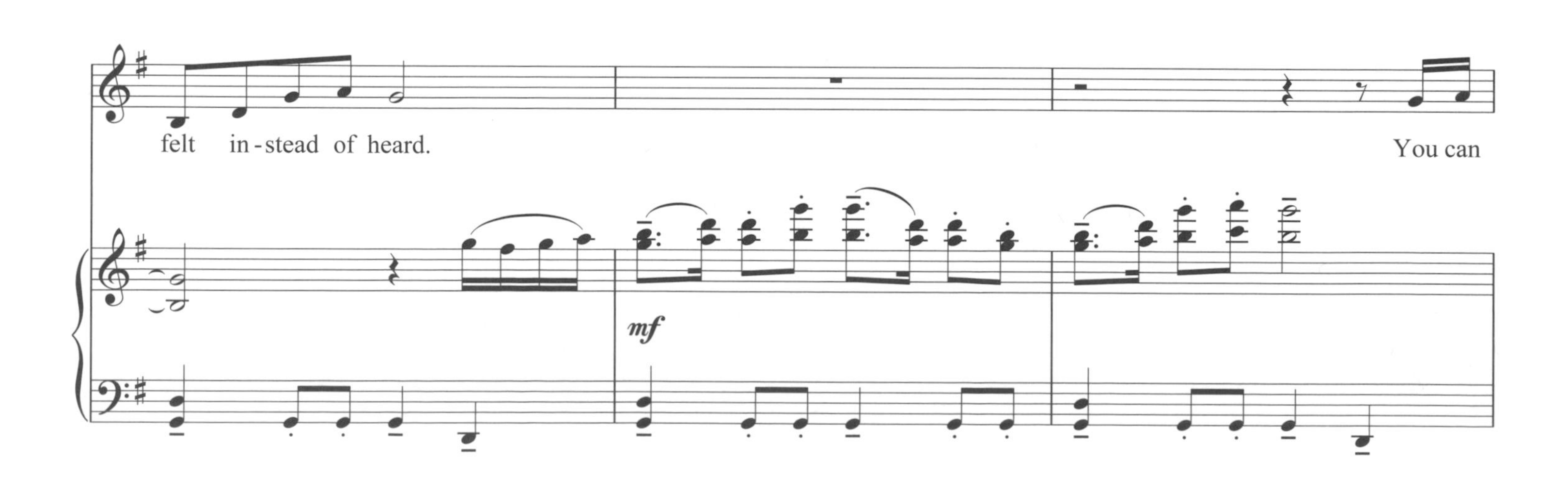

D
Dm
C
Cm
whis - per, sing or shout with - out so much as a word. Try it, go on, like
mp
G
D
so.
mf
8va
3
G
Just let your e - mo - tions tell your bod - y what to do.
mp
mf
Dm
F/G
G7
See how much a sin - gle ges - ture can re - veal! And
tr

C
Em7
A9
C/D
D6
ev - 'ry lit - tle step, ev - 'ry sin - gle step is one step clos - er
C(add2)/D
G
to say - ing what you feel.
6
f
B♭(add2)
Once the mu - sic hits you, in - hi - bi - tions fall a - way. And you find that you're ex - press - ing things your
mf
Fm
B♭9
E♭
E♭m
B♭
E♭/F
F
voice dare - n't say. Don't be a - fraid. Let go!

B♭
Soon as you sur-ren-der what's in - side will sweep on through as the bound-a-ries be tween us dis-ap-
mp
Fm B♭7 E♭ Gm7 C9
pear! And ev-'ry lit-tle step, ev-'ry sin-gle step is
E♭/F Dm/F E♭/F F7 B♭
one step clos - er to talk-ing loud and clear.
p
mp
Dm E♭(add2) B♭(add2)
A dance is like a con-ver - sa - tion ex -
f animated

Eb/G
F7/A
Bb(add2)
Ebmaj7
Bb(add2)/D
cept you nev - er need to make a sound.
And once you've be - gun,
mp
Ebmaj7
Bb(add2)/D
Gm7
Gm7/C
C9
you speak as one, give and take, back and forth, 'round and
D7sus
'round.
Csus2
G/B
Am7(add4)
G
Csus2
G/B
mf

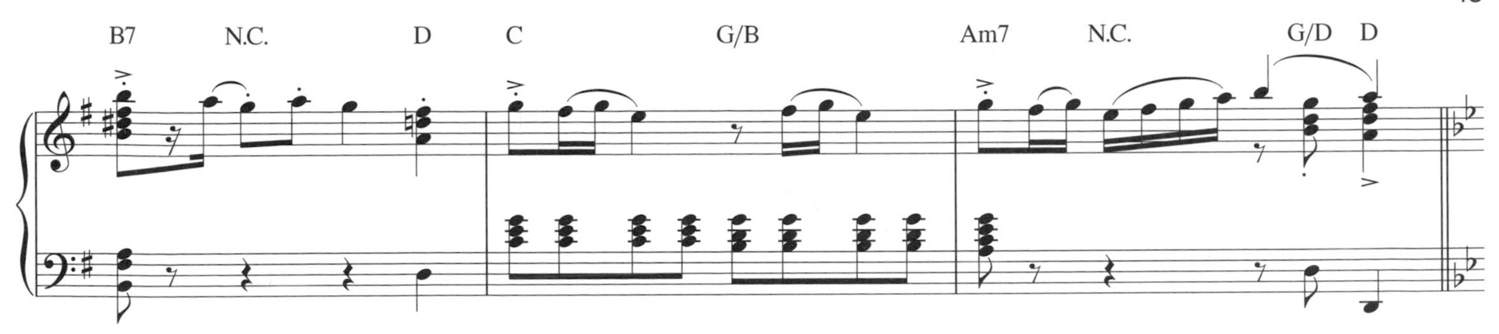
B7 N.C. D C G/B Am7 N.C. G/D D

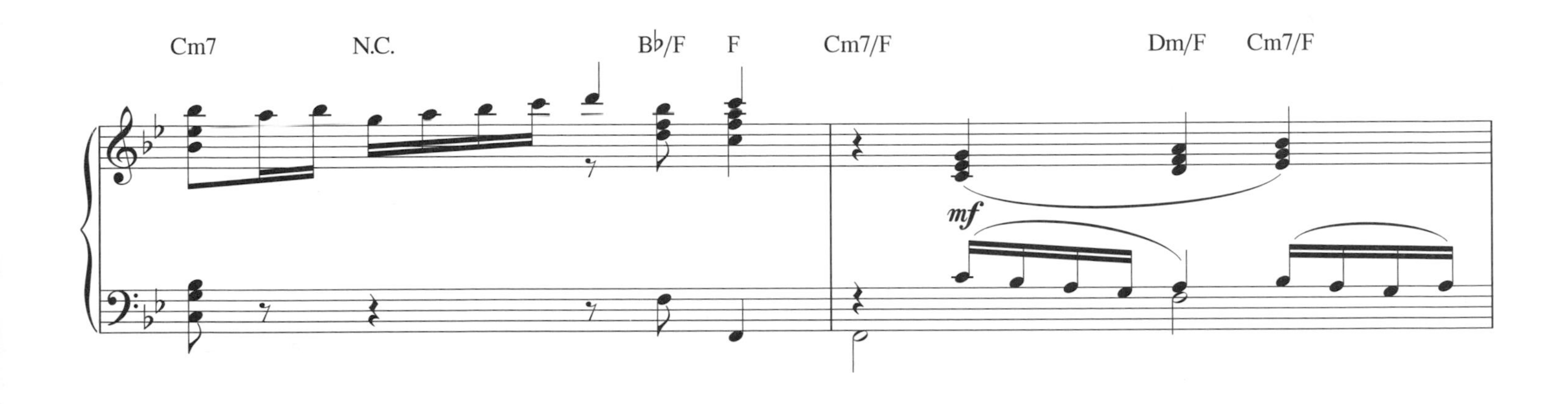
Cm7 N.C. B♭/F F Cm7/F Dm/F Cm7/F
mf

With great passion
Dm/F E♭/F E♭(add2) B♭(add2)/D
poco rall.
A dance is like a con-ver - sa - tion ex -
poco rall.
mf

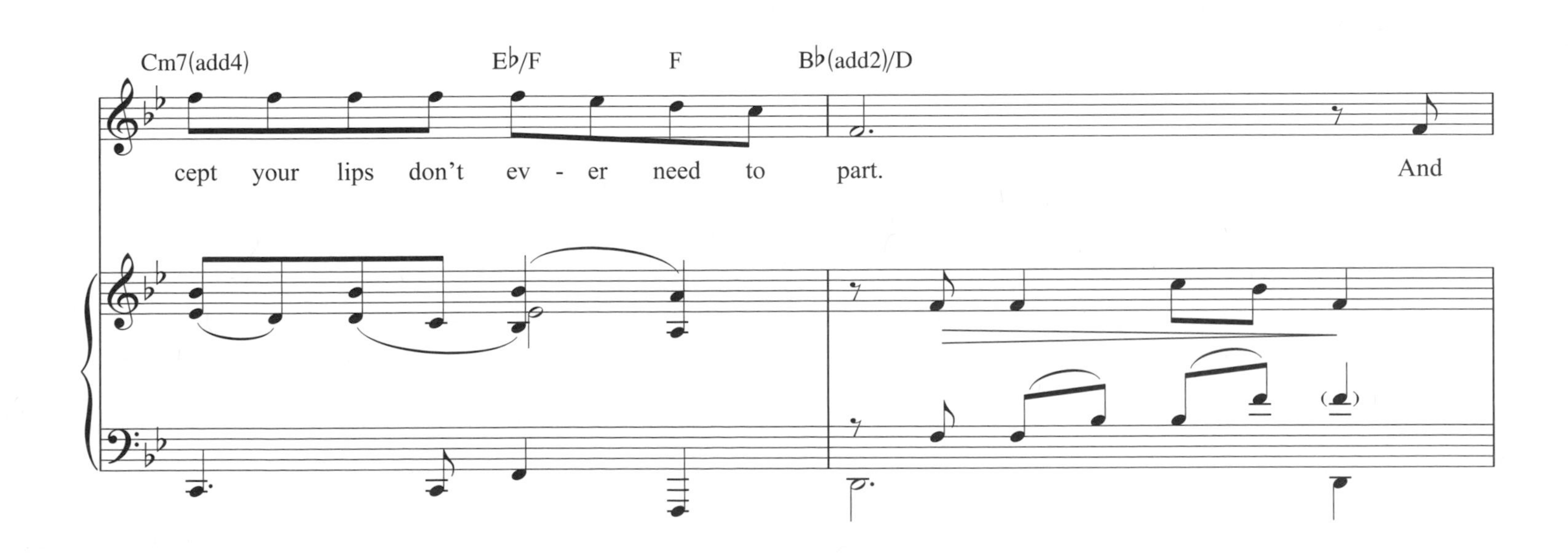
Cm7(add4) E♭/F F B♭(add2)/D
cept your lips don't ev - er need to part. And

E♭maj7 B♭(add2)/D E♭maj7 B♭(add2)/D Gm7
once you've be - gun, you speak as one, cheek to cheek, toe to
mp
Gm7/C C9 C/D D7 D/E E
molto rit.
toe, heart to heart.
molto rit.

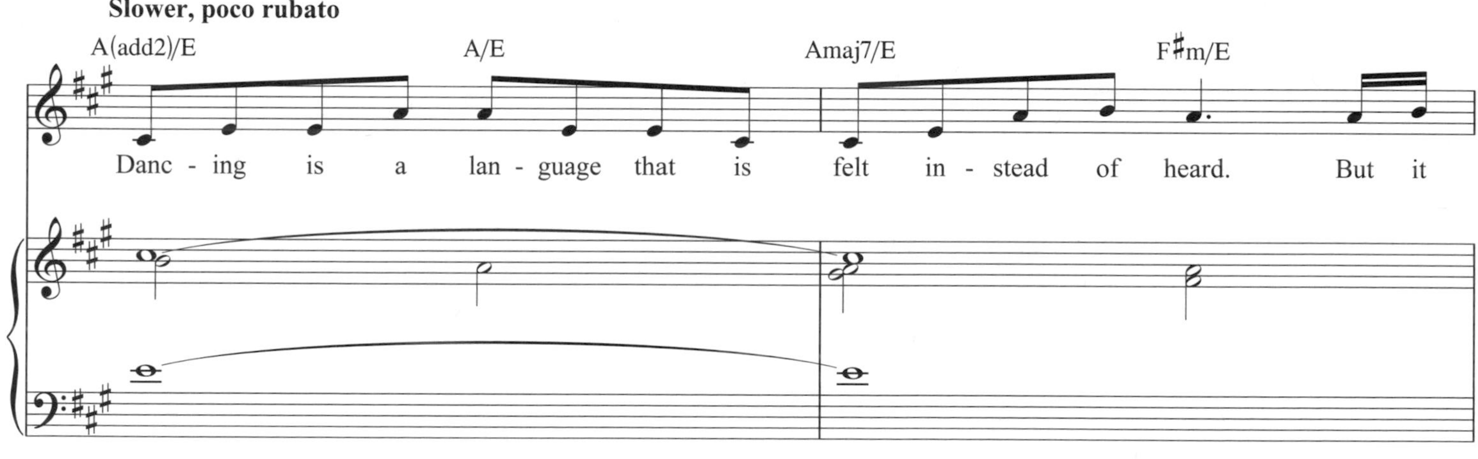
Slower, poco rubato
A(add2)/E A/E Amaj7/E F♯m/E
Danc - ing is a lan - guage that is felt in - stead of heard. But it

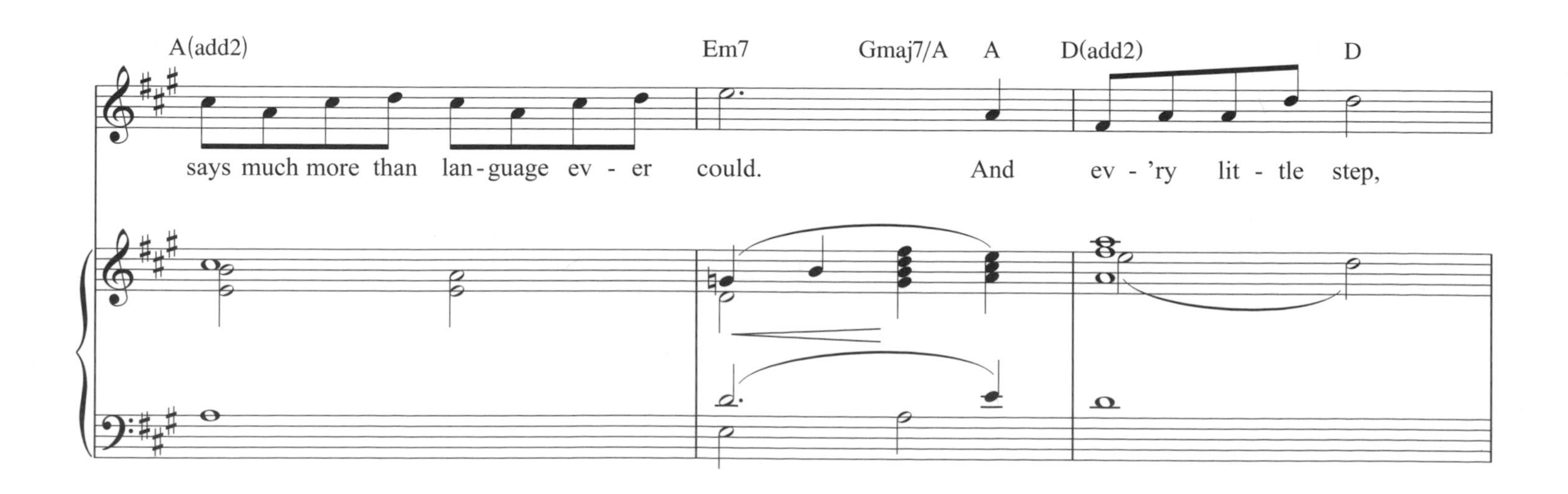
A(add2) Em7 Gmaj7/A A D(add2) D
says much more than lan-guage ev - er could. And ev - 'ry lit - tle step,

Più mosso
F♯m7
A/B
B9
D/E
C♯m/E
D/E
C♯m/E
ev - 'ry sin - gle step is one step clos - er,
p cresc.
Slower
D/E
C♯m/E
E/F♯
F♯7
Bm7
A(add2)/C♯
rit.
one step clos - er,
one step clos - er
mf
rit.
Esus(add2)
A(add2)
Dmaj7
to be - ing un - der - stood.
mp
A
poco rit.

PROUD OF YOUR BOY

from *Aladdin*

Music by Alan Menken
Lyrics by Howard Ashman

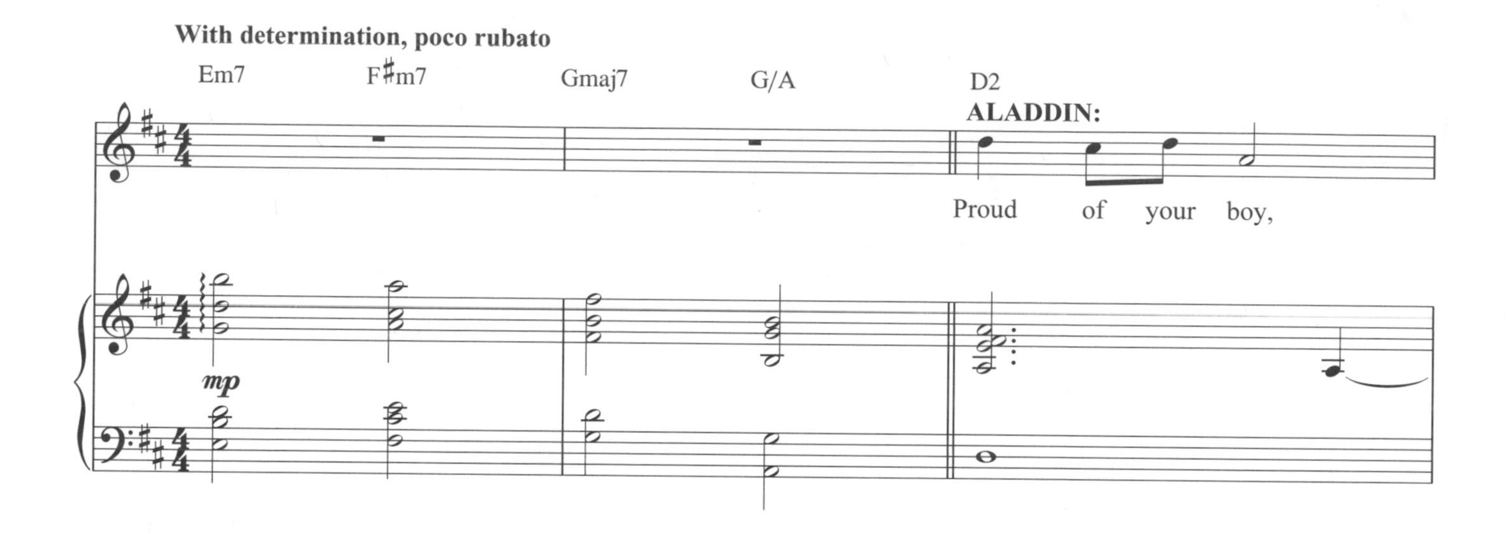

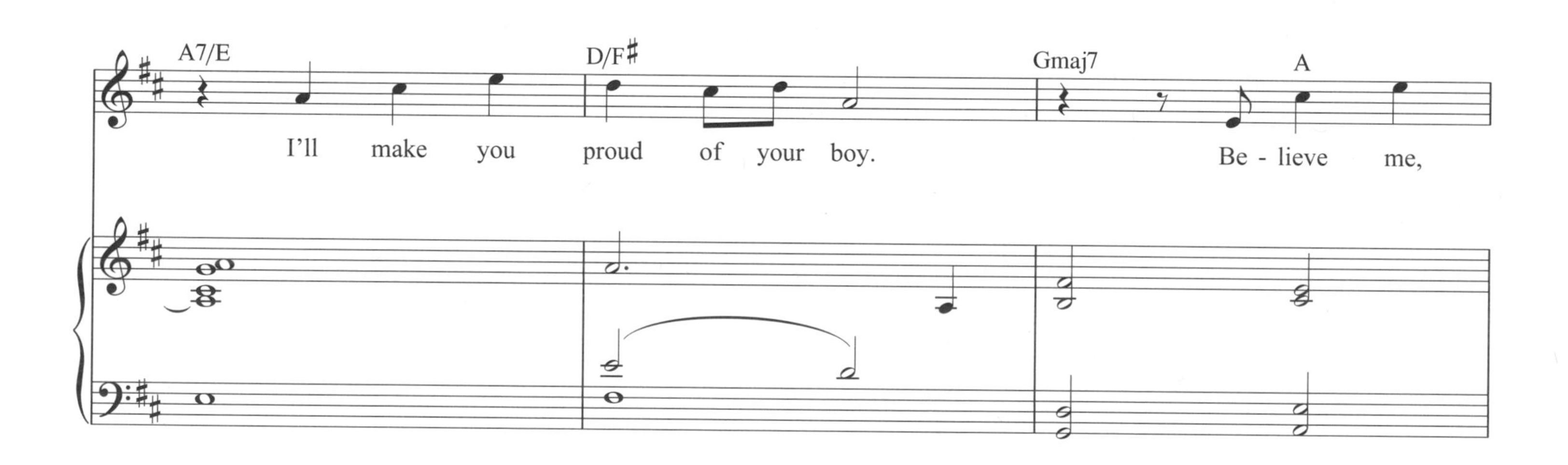

A7
Bm
F♯7/A♯
I've was - ted time,
I've was - ted
Bm/A
G♯m7♭5
Gdim7
D/F♯
me.
So say I'm slow for my age, a late
Bm7
E7
C2
A7sus
A7
bloom - er, o - kay, I a - gree...
that I've been
D
Gmaj7
A7/G
D2/F♯
one rot - ten kid.
Some son, some pride and some joy!

Gmaj7
A7/G
Bm
F♯m/A
G2
D2/F♯
But I'll get o - ver these lous - in' up, mess - in' up, screw - in' up

E7sus
E7
G6
times. You'll see, Ma, now comes the bet - ter part.

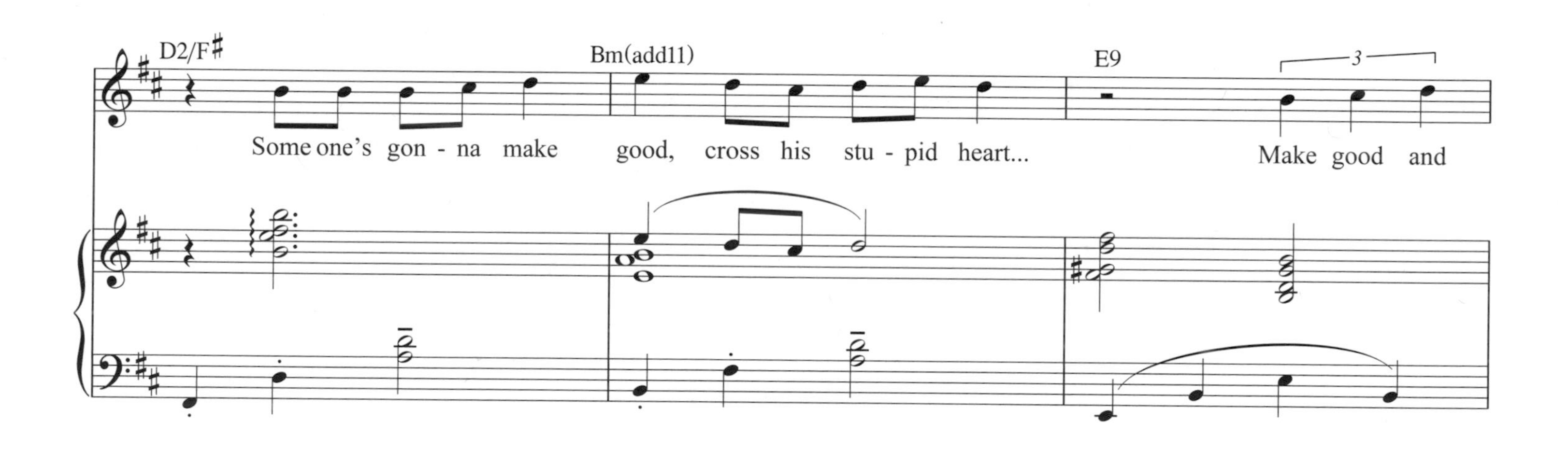
D2/F♯
Bm(add11)
E9
Some one's gon - na make good, cross his stu - pid heart... Make good and

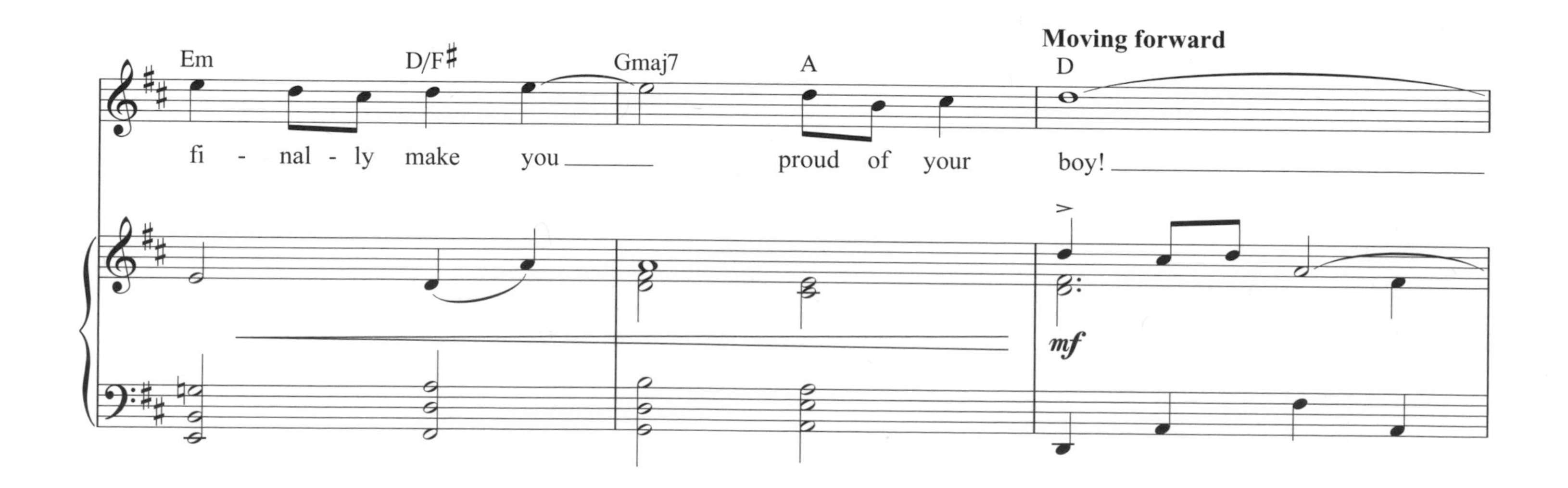
Moving forward
Em
D/F♯
Gmaj7
A
D
fi - nal - ly make you proud of your boy!
mf

A7sus/E
A7/E
D2/F♯
Gmaj7
A
poco rit.
poco rit.
Poco più mosso
G
A/G
Tell me that I've been a louse and a loaf - er, you won't get a fight here, no
mp
D2/F♯
F
G/F
ma'am. Say I'm a gold - brick, a goof - off, no good, but that
C2/E
Am9sus
Am
could - n't be all that I am. Wa - ter flows un - der the
mf

D7sus
D7
G
bridge, let it pass, let it go.
8va
Bm7
E7sus
E7
Em7/A
molto rall.
There's no good rea - son that you should be - lieve me, not yet, I
molto rall.
A tempo, grandly
D
A7sus
A7
know, but... Some - day and soon, I'll make you
f
D/F♯
Gmaj7
A
Bm
F♯m/A
proud of your boy. Though I can't make my - self tall - er or

G6/9
D/F♯
E7sus
E7
smart - er or hand - some or wise. I'll do my
G6
D2/F♯
Bm7(add11)
poco rit.
best, what else can I do? Since I was - n't born per - fect like Dad or you
mf
poco rit.
Freely
E9
Em7
F♯m7
Gmaj7
G/A
poco rit.
Mom, I will try to, try hard to make you proud of your
mp
poco rit.
D
Gmaj7
A
D
a tempo
poco rit.
boy!
a tempo
poco rit.
p

SANTA FE
from *Newsies The Musical*

Music by Alan Menken
Lyrics by Jack Feldman

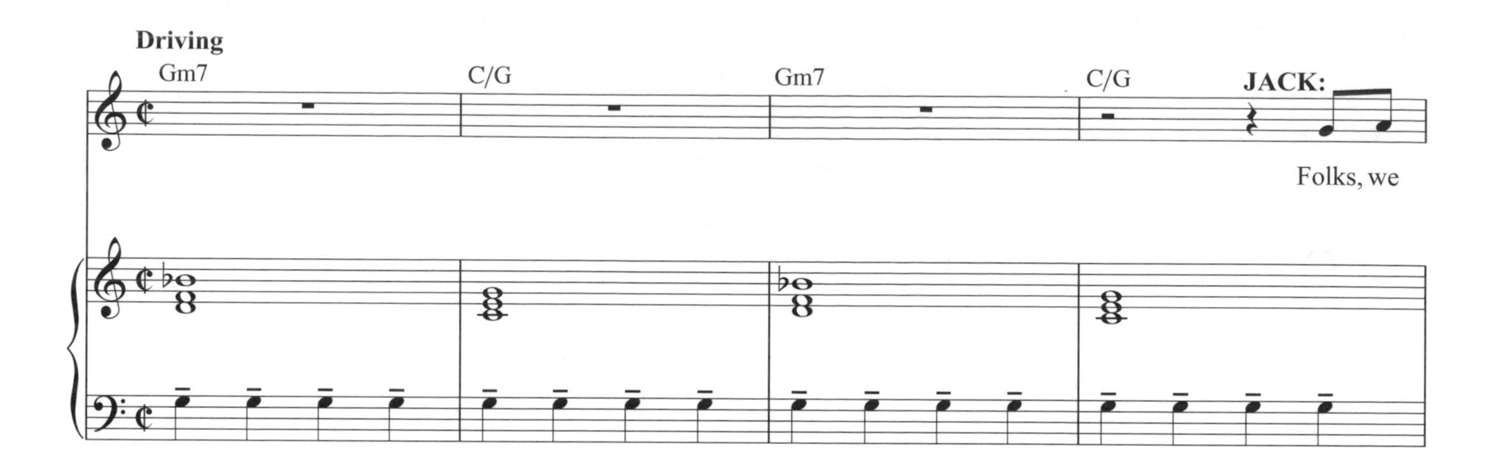

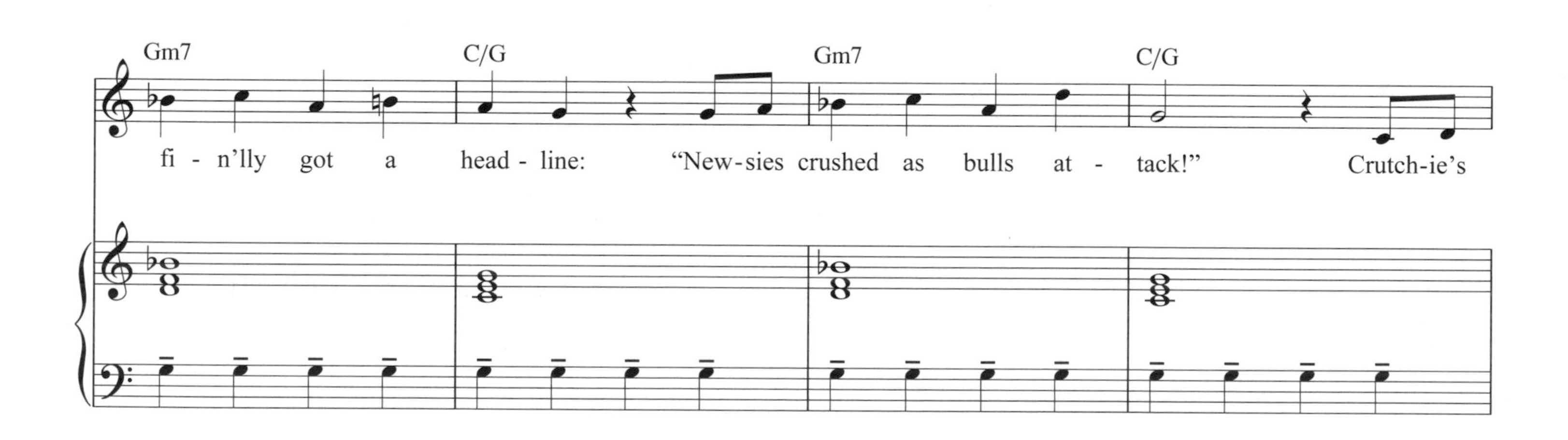

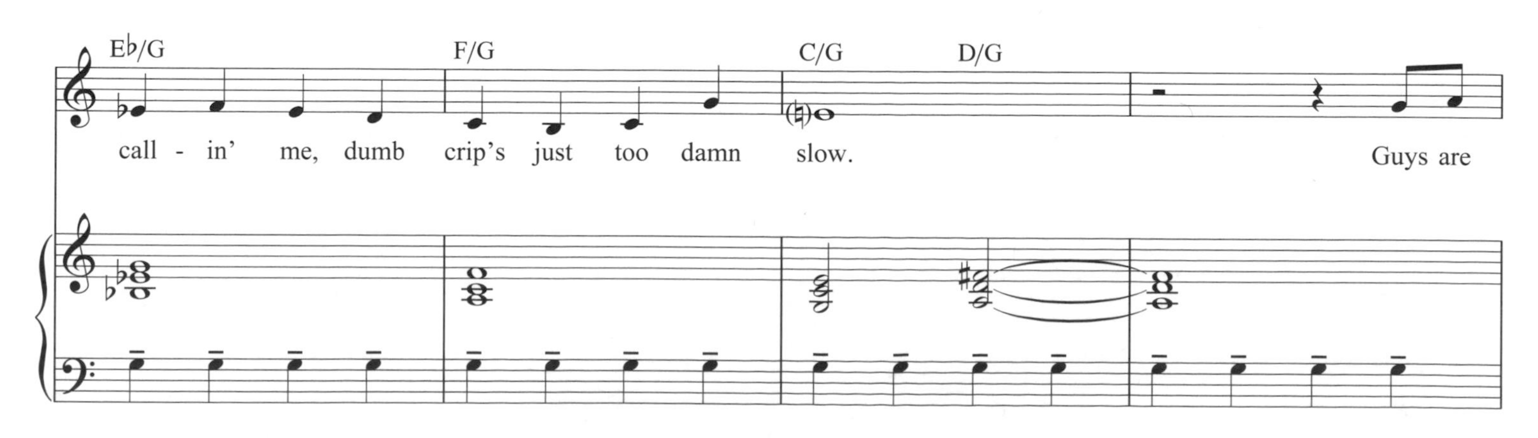

Gm7
C/G
Gm7
C/G
fight - in', bleed - in', fall - in'. Thanks to good ol' Cap - tain Jack. Cap-tain
C/D
D9
B♭(add2)
Jack just wants to close his eyes and go... Let me
sfz
Passionately, more freely
C
Am
F
G/F
F/C
C
go far a - way, some-where they won't nev - er find me. And to -
mf
G/B
E/G♯
Am
Am/G
C/E
mor - row won't re - mind me of to - day. when the

Dm7 G7 Em7 Am7 Dm7 G7 Em7 Am7
cit - y's fi - n'lly sleep - in', and the moon looks old and gray, I get
Ebmaj9 Bbmaj9 Am7 D9 G7sus G7
on the train that's bound for San - ta Fe. And I'm
mp
C Am F G/F Dm/C C
gone! And I'm done! No more run - nin', no more ly - in'. No more
mf
G/B E/G# Am Am/G F
fat old men de - ny - in' me my pay. Just a

Dm7 G7 Em7 C/E Fmaj7 G/F E7sus E7
moon so big and yel - low, it turns night right in - to day. Dreams come

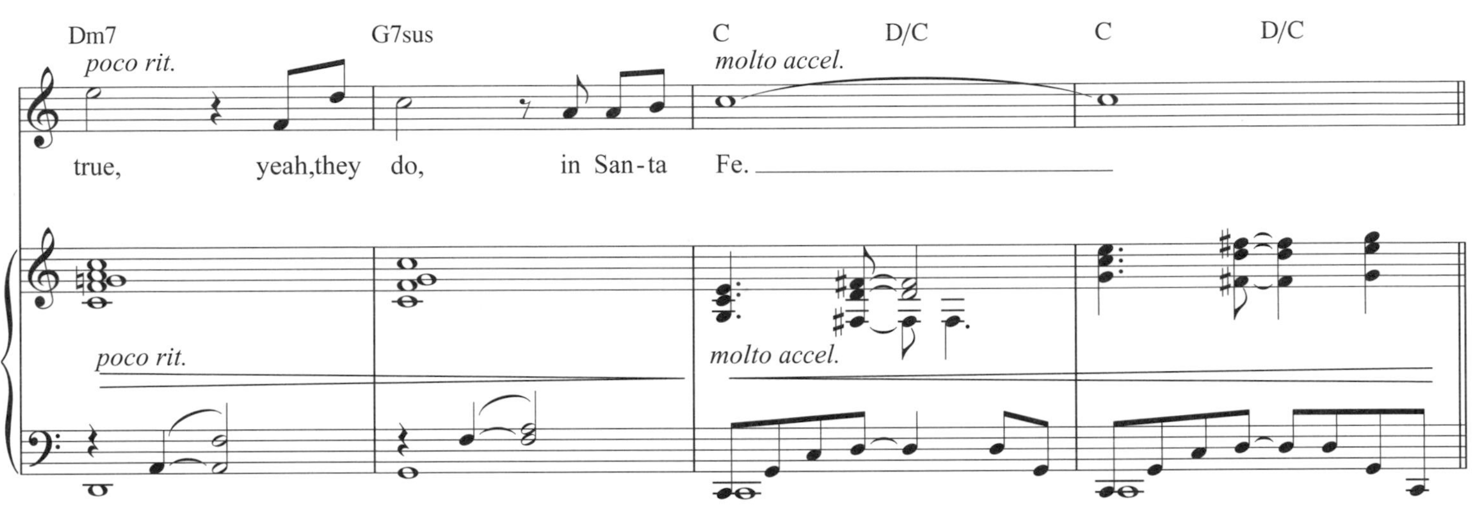
Dm7 G7sus C D/C C D/C
poco rit.
molto accel.
true, yeah, they do, in San - ta Fe.
poco rit.
molto accel.

With more drive
F G/F F G/F Dm/C C Dm/C C
Where does it say you got - ta live and die here?
f

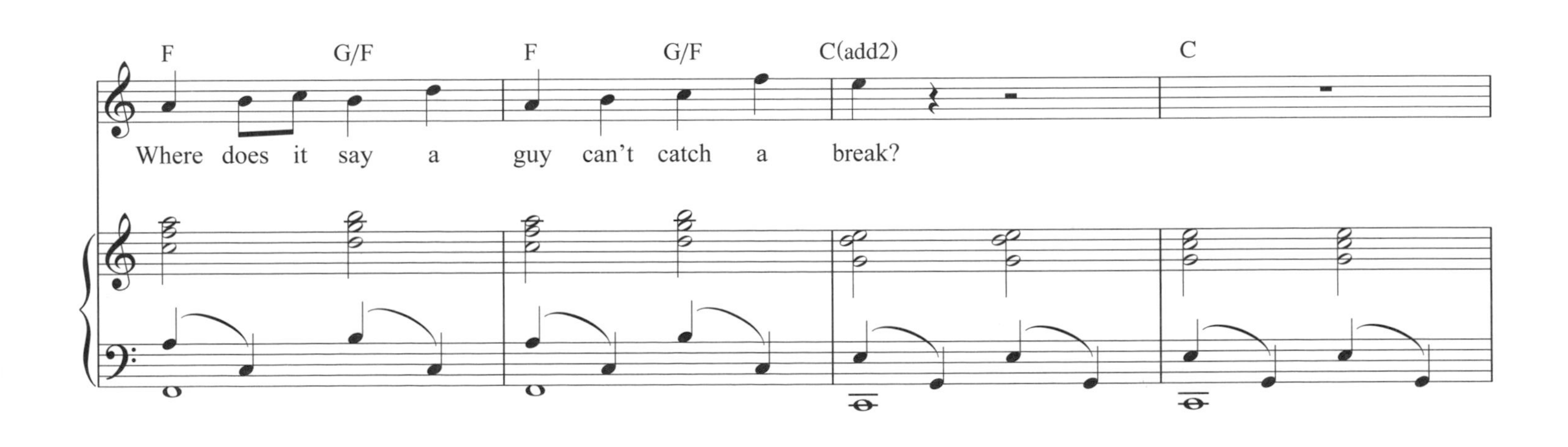
F G/F F G/F C(add2) C
Where does it say a guy can't catch a break?

C/B♭
poco accel.
Am
Why should you on - ly take what you're giv - en? Why should you spend your
poco accel.
Solidly, slightly faster
Fm/A♭
Am(add2)
Fmaj7
whole life liv - in' trapped where there ain't no fu - ture, e - ven at sev - en -
Am(add2)
Fmaj7
teen, break - in' your back for some - one else - 's sake?
B♭(add2)
Bm7♭5
If the life don't seem to suit ya, how 'bout a change of

E7sus
Am(add2)
Am(add2)/G
G/A
scene, far from the lous - y head - lines and the dead - lines in be -
molto rall.
A7
Gmaj7/A
G/A
tween!
molto rall.
A7sus
A7
Broadly, in 4
D
Bm
moving forward
G
A/G
San - ta Fe! My old friend! I can't spend my whole life
ff
G/D
D
A/C♯
F♯/A♯
Bm
Bm/A
G
dream - in', though I know that's all I seem in - clined to do.

D/F♯
Em7
A7
F♯m7
D/F♯
Gmaj7
A7/G
I ain't get - tin' an - y young - er, and I wan - na start brand
F♯7sus
F♯7
More Broadly
Em9
Gmaj7/A
D
F♯m/C♯
new. I need space, and fresh air. Let 'em laugh in my face, I don't
Bm
rit.
F♯m/A
Gmaj7
A7sus
care. Save my place, I'll be there...
11
A tempo (poco rubato)
A
D/A
E/A
mp

D/A
E/A
F/A
D/A
Just be real is all I'm ask - in', not some
F/A
D/A
Bm/E
G/A
paint - in' in my head. 'Cause I'm dead if I can't count on you to -
Bm
Bm/A
rall.
B♭
B♭/A
Gm7
F♯m/A
A
day. I got noth - in' if I ain't got San - ta
f
Briskly
Bm
Bm11
B♭
molto rall.
C/B♭
D
Fe.
ff
molto rall.
sfz p
ff

TAKE A CHANCE ON ME

from the Stage Musical *Little Women*

Music by Jason Howland
Lyrics by Mindi Dickstein

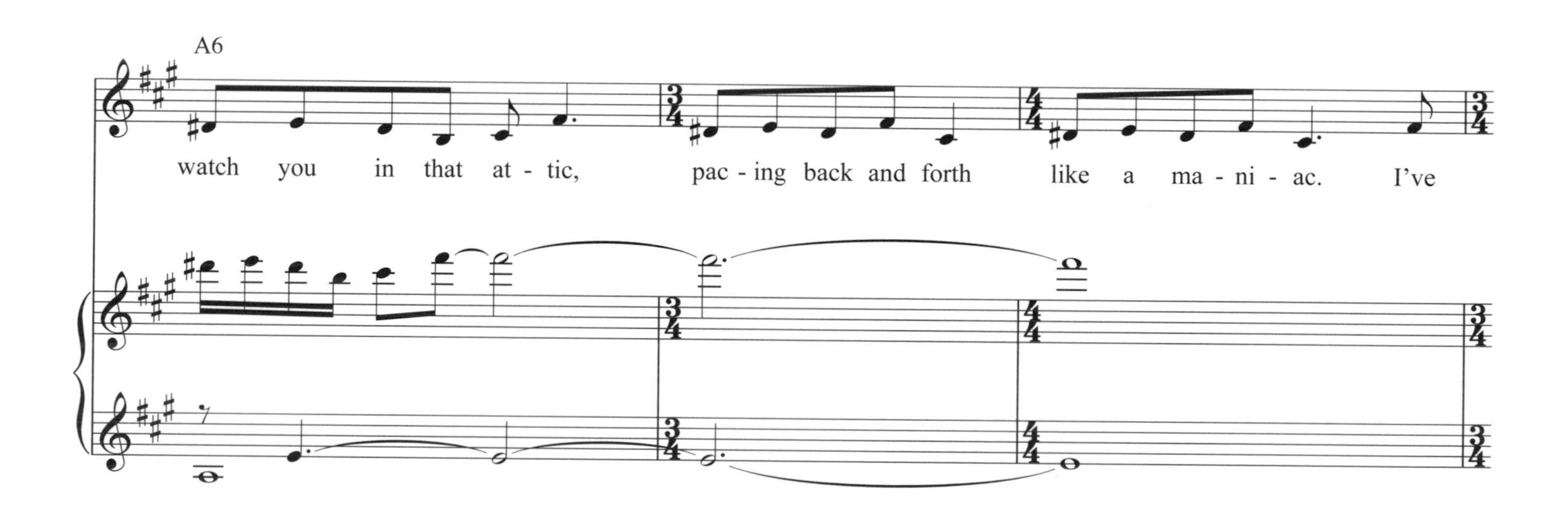

Bm7(add4)
This is ver - y nice, such a love - ly par - ty. The mu - sic sounds so thrill - ing.

G6/9
It makes a per - son feel like danc - ing.

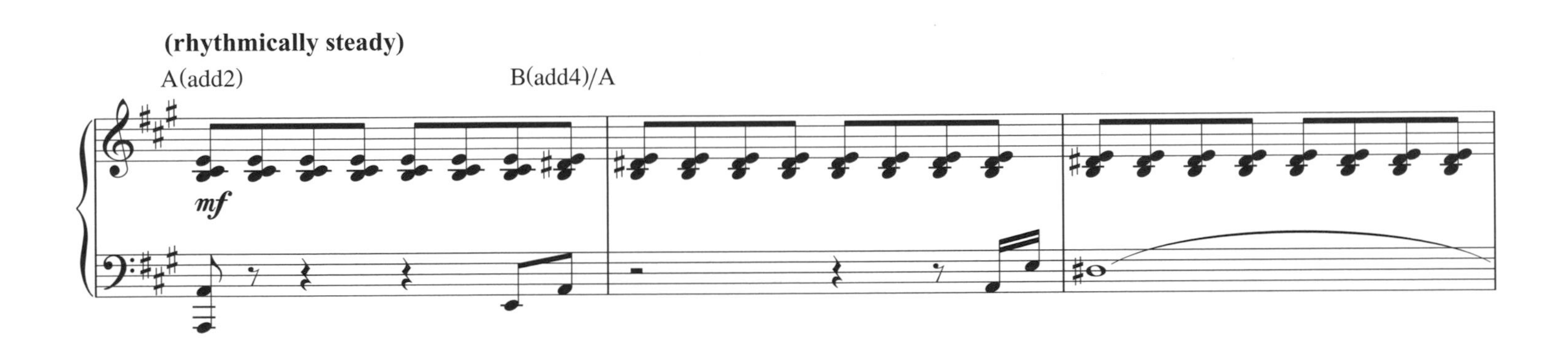
(rhythmically steady)
A(add2)
B(add4)/A
mf

A(add2)
B(add4)/A

G/C D/E A(add2) B(add4)/A
We could do a
Bm(add4)/A A(add2) G/C D/E
hun - dred things, do an - y - thing you please.
A(add2) B(add4)/A Bm7(add4) C#m7
We could fly on gold - en wings a - cross the sev - en seas.
F#7 Bm7(add4) Asus2/C# D6/9
I'll bet we could get a cam - el through a nee - dle if you'll

G/C D D/G D/E A(add2) B(add4)/A Bm(add4)/A G/C Bm7/E
take a chance on me.
A(add2) B(add4)/A Bm(add4)/A A(add2)
We could catch a thou - sand stars and stand them on a pin.
G/C D/E A(add2) B(add4)/A
We could leap from here to Mars and
Bm7(add4) C#m7 F#7 Bm7(add4) Asus2/C# D6/9
make the plan - ets spin. If you want to do all the things you've ev - er

G/C
D
D/G
D/E
A(add2)
B(add4)/A
A/B
dreamed of, come on, take a chance on me.
F#m/B
A(add9)
We could be such friends.
Emaj9/G#
C#m9
A6/9
Friends are nev - er lone - ly. All I know is books.
E(add9)/G#
C#m7(add4)
Books are sol - i - tar - y. But I

F♯m7(add4)
E(add9)/G♯
C♯m9
see you ev - 'ry day,
how you live in your own way,
Dmaj9
and you make me want to dare
3
B7sus
E(add2)
F♯(add4)/E
to take a chance on you.
G♭(add2)
A♭(add4)/G♭
We could live a

A♭m(add4)/G♭
G♭(add2)
E/A B/C♯
mil - lion dreams, but on - ly if we dare.
G♭(add2)
A♭(add4)/G♭
A♭m7(add4)
B♭m7
We could go to such ex - tremes. There's so much we could
E♭7
A♭m7(add4)
G♭sus2/B♭
C♭6/9
share. We'll cir - cle the world do - ing all we've ev - er
A♭m7(add4)
dreamed of. And we'll live in our own way.
8va

Gbmaj7/Bb
Ebm9
And I'll see you ev - 'ry day.
3
Fbmaj9
We'll be the best of friends
Db7sus
Abm7/Db
Gb(add2)
Ab7(add4)/Gb
when you take a chance on me!
E/A B/A Db7sus
Gb

WHAT DO I NEED WITH LOVE

from *Thoroughly Modern Millie*

Music by Jeanine Tesori
Lyrics by Dick Scanlan

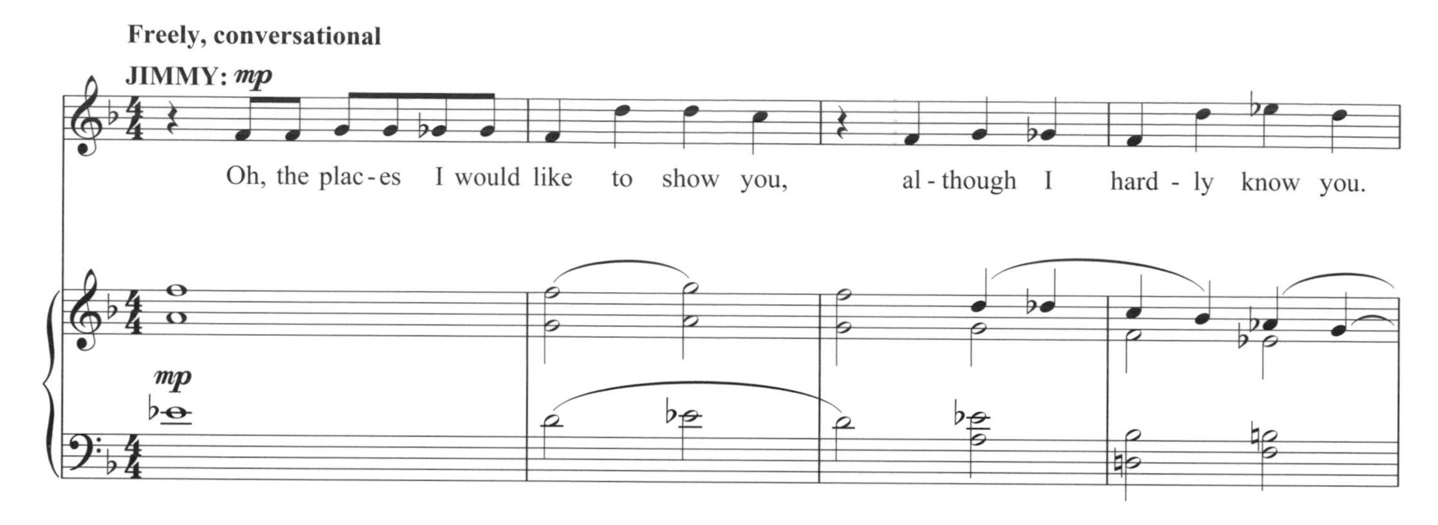

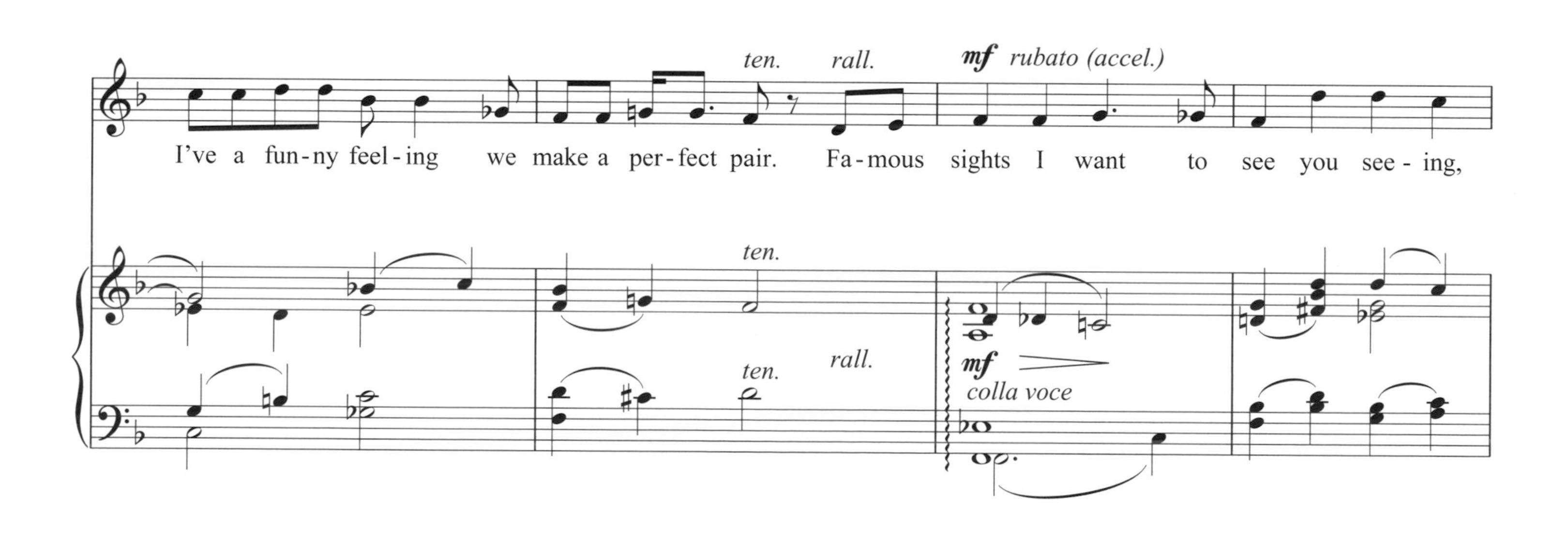

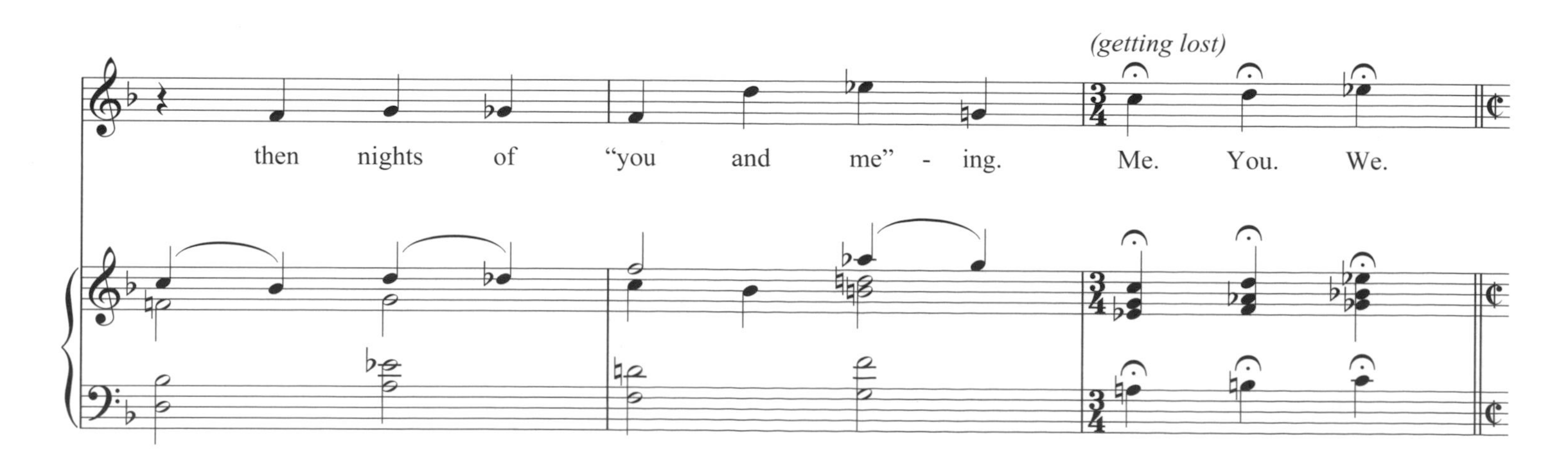

Wait a minute!
Just a minute!
No! No! No! No!
sfz

A tempo - swingy, in 2
I'm a Joe with just one aim:
Ev-'ry night to date a dif-f'rent dame,
mf

Call each one of 'em the same pet name, "Hey, Ba - by."

In a row I have my ducks.
Loads of gals to give me loads of yucks.

Leave the coo - ing to the oth - er clucks. I don't mean may - be.
mp
Got it good. What do I need with love?
3
Al - ways prac - tice what I preach: keep temp - ta - tion out of eas - y reach.
8va
mp
Stick to dolls who wash their hair in bleach, I'm hap - py.
8va
mf

Come and go the way I choose.
Nev - er gon - na sing the
8va
tied down blues.
Oth - er guys would kill to fill my shoes.
No
wing - clipped sap - py!
Got it good.
What do I need with
love?
That was a near miss.
p
f

Talk a-bout a close shave.
Flirt - ed with dis-as - ter.
heavenly
There must be some - one up there watch-in' o - ver me!
mp (straight 8ths)
Talk a-bout a four-leaf - clo - ver-me.
Pe - ter Rab-bit's
mf (swing 8ths)
miss-ing foot - sie means I roll with-out a toot - sie.
mf

Got it good. What do I need with love?
f

I got it good. What do I need with
mf

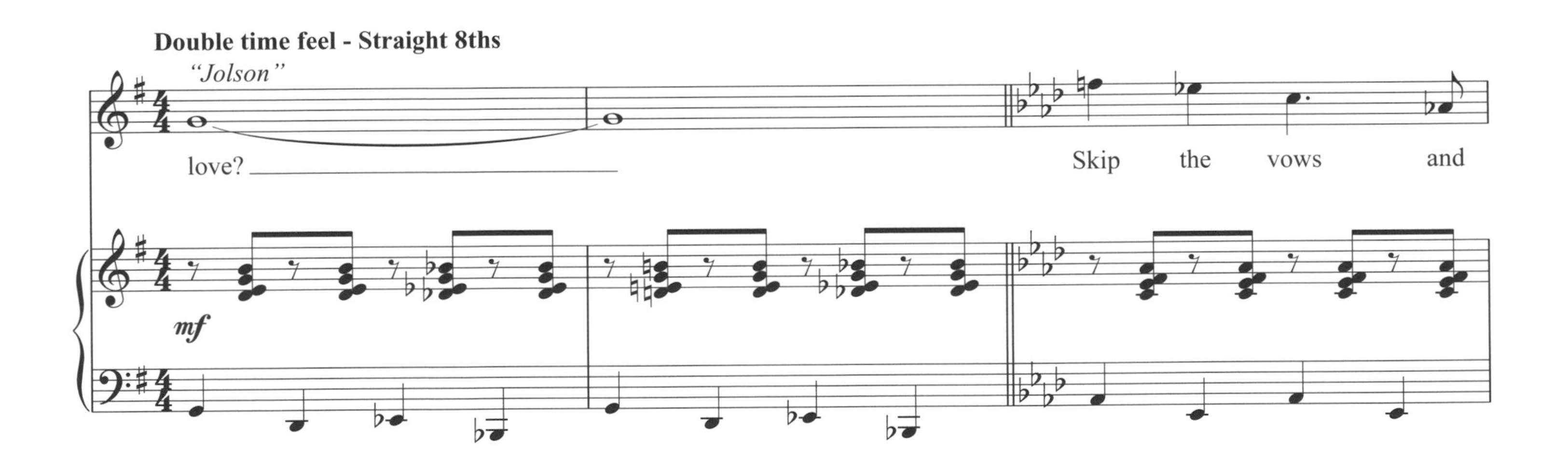
Double time feel - Straight 8ths
"Jolson"
love? Skip the vows and
mf

all that rot. Tell the min - is - ter that "I do" not.

Bright and breez - y is the… Birds and bee - sy is the… Free and eas - y is the
life I got with - out her.
p
ppp
una corda
Freely, slowly
rit.
Al - though I hard - ly know you…
p
p gently
Swing!
f
3
What do I need with love? I
f a tempo

got it good.
Got it good.
I got it
bad!
ff
f
sfzp
3

WAVING THROUGH A WINDOW

from *Dear Evan Hansen*

Music and Lyrics by Benj Pasek
and Justin Paul

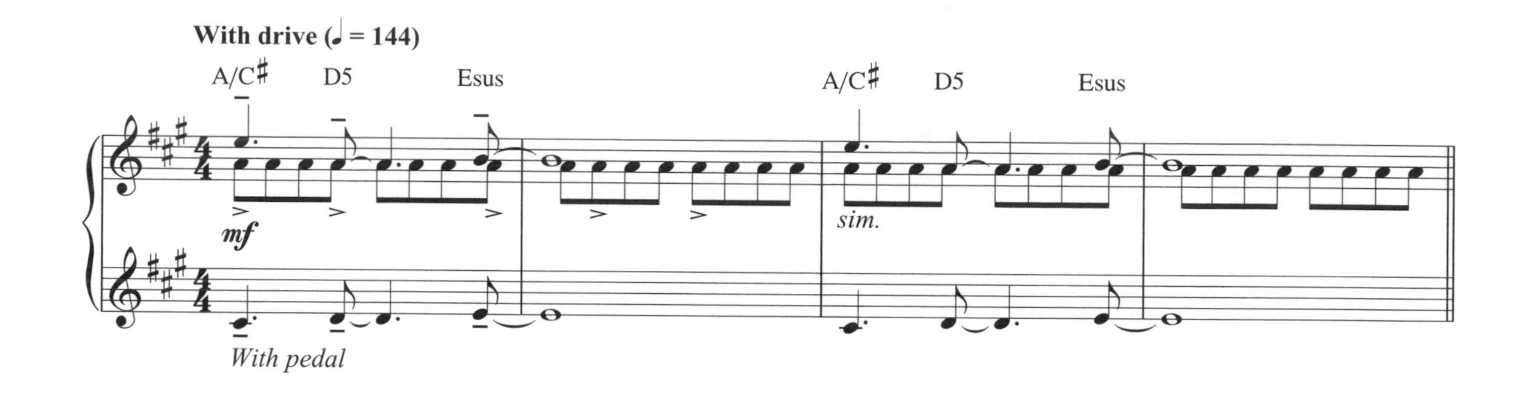

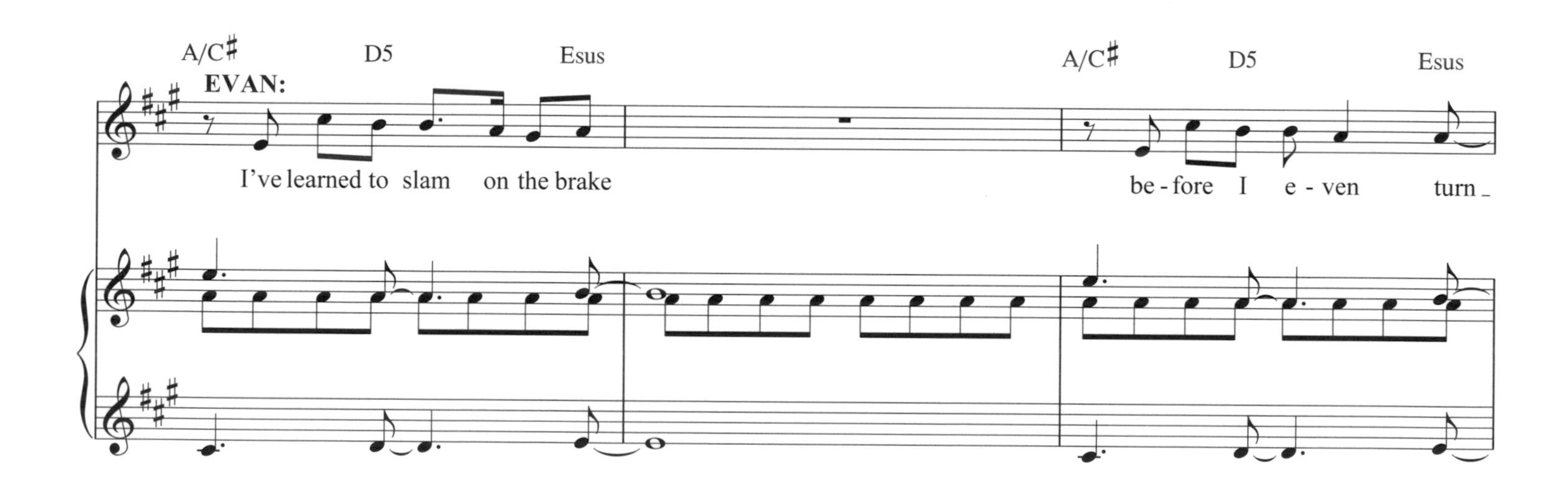

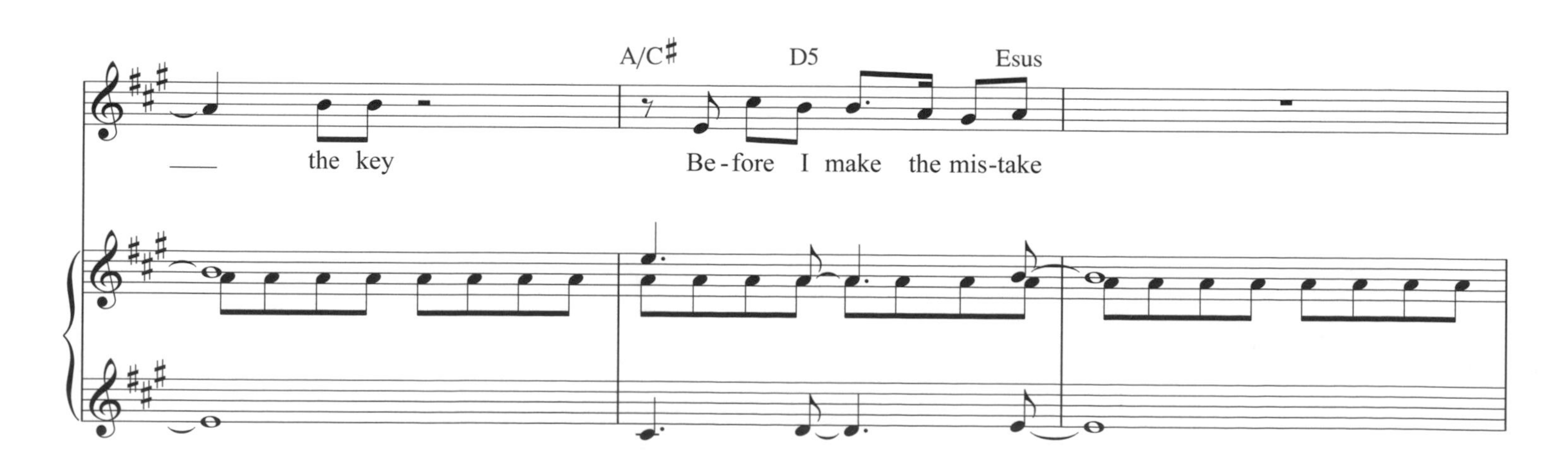

A/C♯
Dsus2
F♯m/C♯
E(add4)
D5
Esus
Be-fore I lead with the worst of me
Give them no rea-son to stare
No slip-pin' up if you slip a-way
So I got noth-in' to share
No, I got noth-in' to say
E(add4,no5)
Bm7(add4)
F♯m7
Step out, step out-ta the sun if you keep

D(add2)
Bm7(add4)
get - tin' burned
Step out, step
F♯m7
E(add4,no5)
A/C♯
D(add2)
E(add4)
out - ta the sun
be - cause you've learned,
be - cause you've learned
cresc.
F♯m7(no5)
Dsus2
On the out - side
al - ways look - in' in
Will I
f
mf
A5
E(add4,no5)
F♯m7(no5)
Dsus2
ev - er be more
than I've al - ways been?
'Cause I'm
tap - tap - tap - pin' on the

A5 E(add4,no5) F♯m7
glass Wav - ing through a win - dow I
Dsus2 A5 E(add4)
try to speak but no - bod - y can hear So I wait a - round for an an -
F♯m7 Dsus2
- swer to ap - pear while I'm watch - watch - watch - in' peo - ple pass
A5 E(add4) C♯7/E♯ F♯m7(no5) Dsus2
Wav - ing through a win - dow Oh Can
f mf

A
E(add4)
an - y - bod - y see? Is an - y - bod - y wav - ing
p sub.
f
Dsus2
A5
E(add4)
back at me?
Dsus2
A
Esus
mf
L.H.
cresc.
Lift (♩ = 146)
A/C♯
Dsus2
E(add4,no5)
We start with stars in our eyes
f
mf
secco
A/C♯
Dsus2
E(add4,no5)
We start be - liev - in' that we be - long
A/C♯
Dsus2
E(add4,no5)
But ev-'ry sun does - n't rise
sim.

A/C♯
Dsus2
F♯m
E(add4)
Bm7(add4)
And no one tells you where you went wrong
w/ pedal
F♯m7
E(add4,no5)
A/C♯
D(add2)
Step out, step out-ta the sun if you keep get-tin' burned
mf
Bm7(add4)
Step out, step out-ta the sun be-cause
F♯m7
E(add4,no5)
A/C♯
Dsus2
E(add4)
F♯m7(no5)
Dsus2
you've learned, be-cause you've learned On the out-side
bring out inner melody
f
with very little pedaling

A5
E(add4)
al-ways look-in' in Will I ev-er be more than I've al-ways been? 'Cause I'm
8vb
F♯m7(no5)
Dsus2
A5
E(add4)
tap - tap - tap-pin' on the glass Wav - ing through a win-
8vb
F♯m7(no5)
D(add2)
- dow I try to speak but no-bod-y can hear So I
8vb
A5
E5
F♯m7(no5)
D(add2)
wait a - round for an an - swer to ap-pear while I'm watch - watch - watch-in' peo-ple
(8vb)

A5
E(add4)
C♯7/E♯
F♯m7(no5)
pass Waving through a window Oh
f
mf
8vb
w/ pedal
Dsus2
A
Can anybody see? Is anybody
E(add4)
A/C♯
Dsus2
Esus
F♯m7(no5)
waving When you're fallin' in a forest and there's nobody around do you
p sub.
f
p legato
A/C♯
Dsus2
Esus
F♯m7(no5)
A/C♯
Dsus2
E(add4,no5)
ever really crash or even make a sound? When you're fallin' in a forest and there's
sim.

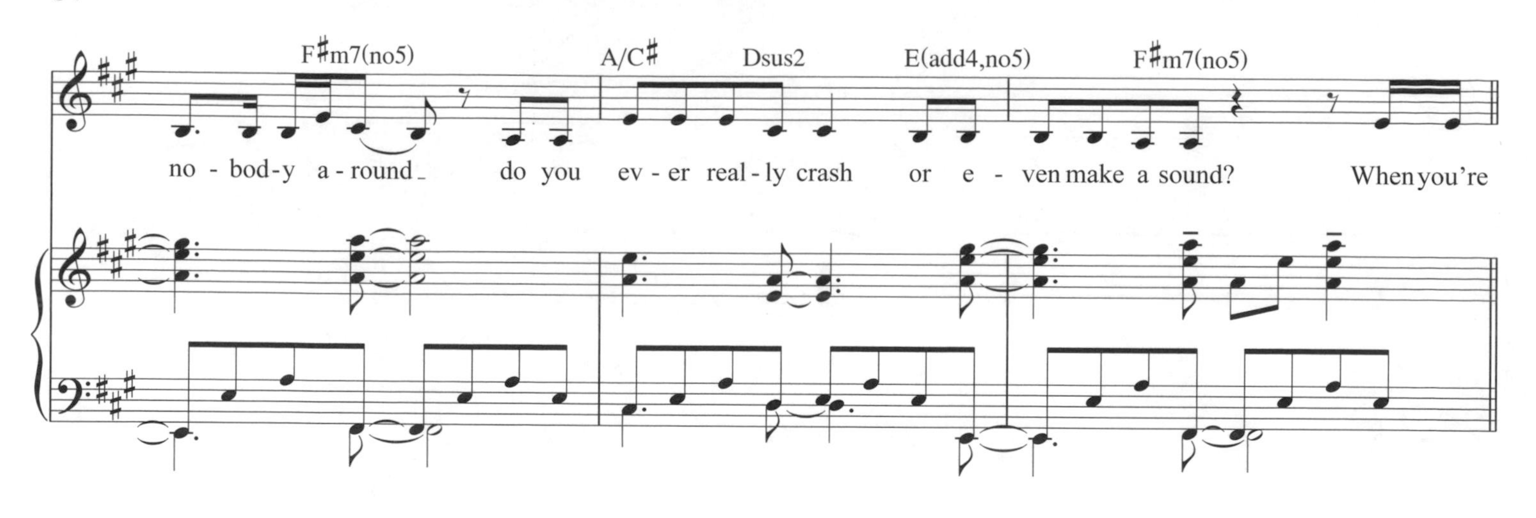

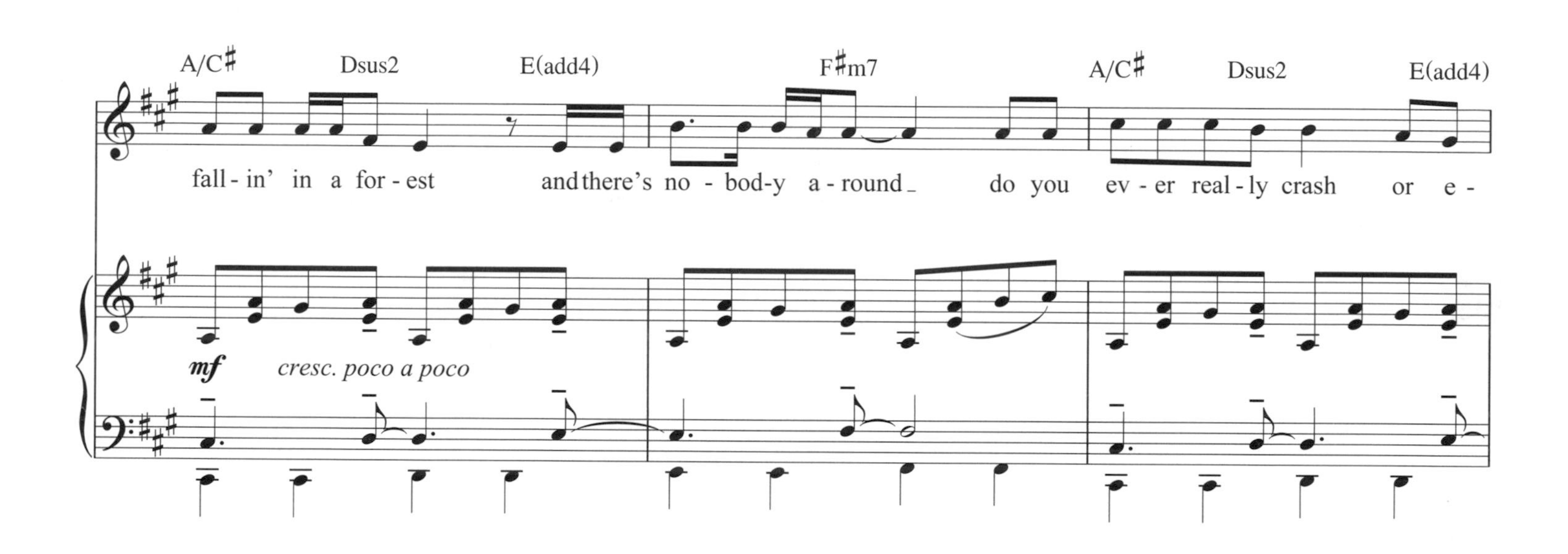

*The company may be omitted when performing this song as a solo.

A/C♯
Dsus2
E(add4)
F♯m7
A/C♯
Dsus2
Esus
ev - er real - ly crash or e - ven make a sound? Did I e - ven make a sound? Did I
Oh
Ah
Oh
f
F♯m7(no5)
A/C♯
Dsus2
Esus
N.C.
Gm7(no5)
e - ven make a sound? It's like I nev - er made a sound Will I ev - er make a sound?
Oh
Oh
Ah
Oh
sfz
ff
E♭sus2
B♭5
F(add4)
On the out - side al - ways look - in' in Will I ev - er be more
Oh

Gm7(no5)
E♭sus2
than I've al-ways been? 'Cause I'm tap - tap - tap-pin' on the glass
Oh
B♭5
F(add4)
Gm7(no5)
E♭sus2
Wav - ing through a win - dow I try to speak but
Oh
Oh
B♭
F(add4,no5)
no-bod-y can hear So I wait a-round for an an - swer to ap-pear while I'm
Oh
8vb

Gm7(no5)
E♭sus2
B♭
F(add4,no5)
watch - watch - watch-in' peo - ple pass
Wav - ing through a win -
Oh
Oh
8vb
D7/F♯
Gm7(no5)
E♭sus2
B♭
- dow Oh
Can an - y - bod - y see?
sfz
mf
f
F(add4)
B♭/D
E♭(add2)
F(add4)
Is an - y - bod - y wav - ing
back at me?
sub. p
f

B♭/D
E♭(add2)
F(add4)
Is an - y - bod - y wav - ing?
Oh
Oh
Gm7(no5)
B♭5/A
E♭sus2
Wav - ing
Wav - ing
Whoa
Oh
Oh
ff
mf
N.C.
rall.
B♭
B♭sus2
N.C./B♭
whoa
rall.
ff
rall.
ppp
sffz